"In this book, Nina Brown provides hope come the negative impact of self-absorbe to-earth, practical strategies for gaining effect, and developing approaches to overcome it. The information in this book can also be valuable to anyone working with adults trying to understand how their parents still negatively influence them as adults."

> —**Travis J. Courville, LCSW, CGP, FAGPA**, licensed clinical social worker, fellow of the American Group Psychotherapy Association, certified group psychotherapist, and adjunct professor in the Graduate College of Social Work at the University of Houston

"Positive revenge and bypassing forgiveness are two brilliant strategies found in this remarkable guide that provides a detailed map to moving forward from wounds inflicted by parents who prioritize themselves above their children. This novel path can preserve and repair connection without retaliatory damage. Included are varied expressive exercises— writing, drawing, visualizing—that have broad reach for individuals, practitioners, and educators alike. With sensitivity and without judging, Nina Brown outlines how to implement these creative steps to healing that can lead the way to your most satisfying life!"

> —**Helene Satz, PsyD, ABPP, CGP, LFAGPA**, behavioral health faculty at Tripler Army Medical Center in Honolulu, HI; 2018 recipient of the Harold S. Bernard Group Psychotherapy Training Award from the International Board for Certification of Group Psychotherapists

"Excellent reference for anyone, especially children reared by a self-absorbed parent. The book is broken down into digestible bits, making it very easy to absorb. Nina Brown invites the reader to take the path to the person they want to be. All along, I thought I assumed the role of the compliant child; reading this book helped me to realize instead that I assumed the role of the rebellious child—this new perspective has been very helpful."

> —**Nial P. Quinlan, LPC, PhD**, counselor in private practice in Norfolk/Yorktown, VA

Children
of the Self–
Absorbed

THIRD EDITION

A Grown-Up's Guide to Getting Over Narcissistic Parents

Nina W. Brown, EdD, LPC

New Harbinger Publications, Inc.

Publisher's Note

This publication is designed to provide accurate and authoritative information in regard to the subject matter covered. It is sold with the understanding that the publisher is not engaged in rendering psychological, financial, legal, or other professional services. If expert assistance or counseling is needed, the services of a competent professional should be sought.

In consideration of evolving American English usage standards, and reflecting a commitment to equity for all genders, "they/them" is used in this book to denote singular persons.

NEW HARBINGER PUBLICATIONS is a registered trademark of New Harbinger Publications, Inc.

Distributed in Canada by Raincoast Books

Copyright © 2020 by Nina W. Brown
New Harbinger Publications, Inc.
5674 Shattuck Avenue
Oakland, CA 94609
www.newharbinger.com

Cover design by Amy Shoup; Acquired by Elizabeth Hollis Hansen; Edited by Ken Knabb

Library of Congress Cataloging-in-Publication Data

Names: Brown, Nina W., author.
Title: Children of the self-absorbed : a grown-up's guide to getting over narcissistic parents / by Nina W. Brown.
Description: Third edition. | Oakland, CA : New Harbinger Publications, [2020] | Includes bibliographical references.
Identifiers: LCCN 2019055179 (print) | LCCN 2019055180 (ebook) | ISBN 9781684034208 (paperback) | ISBN 9781684034215 (pdf) | ISBN 9781684034222 (epub)
Subjects: LCSH: Parent and adult child. | Adult children--Psychology. | Narcissism. | Families--Psychological aspects.
Classification: LCC HQ755.86 .B76 2020 (print) | LCC HQ755.86 (ebook) | DDC 158.2/4--dc3
LC record available at https://lccn.loc.gov/2019055179
LC ebook record available at https://lccn.loc.gov/2019055180

Printed in the United States of America

24   23   22

10   9   8   7   6   5   4   3

This book is dedicated to our son Michael R. Brown, September 1960–April 2019. We will always love you.

Contents

Preface

When children grow up with a self-absorbed parent, they may find that there are lingering effects on them as adults—effects such as being manipulated, seduced, or intimidated to do things they do not wish to do or that are destructive for them; being unable to initiate and maintain satisfying and enduring relationships; being unable to say no and stick to it; and other negative behaviors and attitudes with others as well as with the self-absorbed parent. Some try to work through their issues or concerns with mental health professionals, but find that it is just about impossible to adequately describe what their formative years were like.

Read the following and see if any of this resonates with you:

> *It's all about you, and you make sure of that. Your wants, needs, and demands are always your main focus.*
> *Everything must be done your way or it's not acceptable. You never stop to consider that others have rights too. In your eyes, you know what is best, you are always right, and I agree with you and do what you want or incur your wrath, displeasure, and disappointment.*
>
> *You are completely self-serving. You use every situation to fulfill your needs. You are blind to others' needs, deaf to their emotions, and expert at manipulation. You work hard to trigger my guilt, sadness, rage, and shame, and to make sure that I am exactly what you want me to be. You constantly berate, blame, and criticize me, and I am always miserable around you.*

I want to please you, but I never seem able to. You are like a hurricane: I know you are coming so I prepare for the damage you can do, but my preparations are in vain. After you leave, I am left with the residual emotions to clean up while you move on, not knowing or caring about any damage you cause me or anyone else.

How I long for some sign that you like and love me, but in all my years with you, I've never felt this, and this lack affects me deeply. You never showed any understanding of what I was feeling, and when I tried to make you understand, you either ignored or minimized my feelings or became angry and said that I was ungrateful or disrespectful for criticizing you.

Now that I am an adult, I find that I still long for your love and know that you cannot be different, but that doesn't take away my yearning for a more satisfying and loving relationship.

Adult children of self-absorbed parents can find it difficult to describe what the parent did that continues to negatively affect them as adults. When they try to tell someone about their experiences, they often do not have the words to convey the impact of the parent's acts on them or to enable them to understand why they felt and reacted as they did and still do. In addition, there may be effects still lingering from when they were infants and in a preverbal stage of development that they cannot retrieve from memory or express in words. These negative effects continue to impact their current well-being and self-esteem, which may in turn impact other aspects of their lives, especially their relationships.

This third edition extends the materials provided in the first two editions of this book to aid readers to better understand the continuing negative effects of a self-absorbed parent on their development and current functioning. Since better understanding alone may not be sufficient, I have also provided suggestions for positive personal changes—actions and strategies that may help them overcome those negative effects and become the person they want to be.

My hope is that this book will encourage and guide you to a better understanding of yourself, your feelings, your reactions, and even some of your actions. There may be some things about yourself that you want to change, and what may emerge as you read through the book may give you some ideas and guidance on how you can make those changes, in order to overcome the negative impact of your self-absorbed parent and to have a more rewarding and fulfilling life.

CHAPTER 1

Infuriating, Critical, Demanding, and Unreasonable Parents

Betsy had lunch with her father to talk about her desire to go back to college and get a degree in English Education so that she could become a teacher. At lunch, her father made it clear that he was not supportive of her becoming a teacher and was insistent that she become an accountant. He was also disparaging of her previous choice of a college major and of her subsequent jobs. He told her that he would be very disappointed if she did not take his advice, since he was more knowledgeable and successful than she was.

Betsy left the lunch feeling defeated and demoralized. She wished that she could tell her father that he always made everything about him—his wants, needs, and demands. He insists that everything be done his way or it isn't acceptable that he knows what is best for others and never considers their perspectives. Whenever Betsy didn't do what her father wanted, he was angry and withheld his approval of her.

Do you feel that the title of this chapter describes your parent? Do you long for your parent to accept you as you are instead of trying to make you into your parent's image of what you should be?

Do you feel that your parent was not understanding or empathic most of the time when you were growing up?

Does your parent make you feel responsible for their emotional or psychological or physical well-being?

Does your parent constantly berate, blame, and criticize you?

Are you miserable when you are around your parent?

Are you still longing for your parent's love and approval even as an adult?

If your answer to many of these questions is yes, then you may have grown up with a parent whose behaviors and attitudes were symptomatic of being self-absorbed.

Like most other readers of this book, you may realize that your childhood experiences are continuing to exert unwanted and negative effects on you as an adult, and you want to do something to minimize or eliminate those effects. The first edition of *Children of the Self-Absorbed* described the actions and attitudes of parents that have a destructive, narcissistic pattern of behaviors, although those parents might not necessarily be categorized as narcissists. The second edition provided additional understanding of self-absorbed parents' early and continuing influences on their children who are still affected by them as adults. The primary emphasis was on how those adults could facilitate their recovery from their parents' negative influences.

This new edition adds discussions and presentations that may answer some of your questions about all of those topics, as well as suggestions for how to overcome their negative effects. The material is written for those who, as adults, may be still trying to heal some of the injuries to their inner essential selves, and to recognize how some of these early negative parental influences may still affect their current relationships. This edition also provides avenues that can be used to help you find your potential and possibilities for getting out from under the continuing impact and influences of a self-absorbed parent.

Central are the five following guiding thoughts and principles:

- You may have suffered numerous parental empathic failures that affected your psychological growth and development and that also continue to affect you today.

- You felt or feel that you are responsible for the parent's emotional, psychological, or physical well-being and have worked hard to achieve this without success or the parent's appreciation.

- Your current self-esteem, self-confidence, and self-efficacy are not at the levels you feel they should be. Your relationships may also be affected.

- Your efforts to try to get your parent to see your perspective, to approve of you, or to show you love and appreciation have been futile.

- Nothing you did or tried to do to get the parent to change has been successful. The parent did not and will not change.

Among the new topics in this edition are the following:

- A deeper understanding of why some self-absorbed parents may be very successful in other parts of their lives, and why others do not see their self-absorption.

- How to limit or eliminate your cooperation with your parent if that cooperation continues to erode your self-confidence, self-esteem, and self-efficacy.

- How to give up surviving and learn to thrive.

- The benefits of positive revenge and how to get it.

- How to become more mindful of how to help yourself heal from early parental negative effects.

- How to give up the fantasy that the parent will change.

- How to prevent the negative effects of the parent's dismissive and demeaning attitudes.

- How to capitalize on your strengths and unrecognized inner resources.

As you read and work through the activities provided, you can expect to have some difficult memories triggered. Repressed and suppressed long-standing issues and concerns may emerge into awareness, including unfinished matters from the past that were never fully or satisfactorily resolved. Although you probably don't relish the idea of having these thoughts and feeling these emotions, doing so is a necessary first step in understanding your experience and beginning the process of change. Change can be difficult, but this book offers guidance for minimizing or eliminating the negative effects of parental self-absorption. You don't have to continue to suffer and be frustrated. As you read, you will find that there are ways that you can help yourself with:

- Interactions with the parent and triggered negative feelings.

- Thoughts about your essential inner self and other basic attitudes.

- Relationships with the parent and with others.

- Your ability to manage difficult events and situations.

I encourage you to use the activities in this book to gain greater awareness and understanding, and to adopt those suggested strategies that best fit your personality.

Narcissism Defined

The term "narcissism" has been used quite a bit so far. Narcissism can be defined as self-love, self-esteem, and other similar feelings about the inner essential self, and this is the definition that forms the framework for what is applied and described about adults in this book. Consider adult narcissism as being located on a continuum. On one end, there is healthy adult narcissism that is mature and realistic (Kohut 1977). On the other end, there is pathological narcissism that is extremely immature, very unrealistic, and completely self-serving. In between the two ends lies undeveloped narcissism, where some aspects of the person have progressed to the healthy end, some may still be in the immature range, and still others are in the process of developing. Think of the immature range as that which contains behaviors and attitudes that are expected of infants and children but that signal immaturity and undeveloped narcissism in adults, such as constantly boasting or bragging, expecting others to immediately meet one's demands without protest, or taking unnecessary risks that can be very self-destructive.

Many, if not most, adults have some developed narcissism and some that is undeveloped, as well as some that may not be on either end of the continuum, neither full pathological nor fully developed and healthy. The self-absorption or narcissism discussed in this book is where the person exhibits many of the behaviors and attitudes of the person with the diagnosis of Narcissistic Personality Disorder (NPD) as described in the American Psychiatric Association's Diagnostic and Statistical Manual of Mental Disorders (DSM-5), but it is *not* an NPD. We will be concerned primarily with the self-absorbed parent's observable behaviors and attitudes, and how these may have impacted you then and even now, and how you can heal, grow, and develop to become the person you want to be.

This definition of narcissism is not evaluative or judgmental—it is simply descriptive of a collection of behaviors and attitudes that reveal how people perceive and feel about their self, about others, and about their degree of separateness from others. We will focus on these revealing behaviors and attitudes and begin to understand the impact of these on relationships, how their growth and development are lacking, and how this lack of growth and development is unconscious and not known to that person. It is the last point that can present difficulties for others in a relationship, because persons with immature or undeveloped narcissism are unaware that they exhibit behaviors and attitudes reflective of an earlier stage of development and tend to be oblivious of the impact these have on others.

The information and strategies you will find in this book can be of enormous help to you in your interactions with your parent and in your everyday life. But no book can take the place of working with a competent mental health professional who can guide your personal development. That work can produce the deep understanding and personal changes you may desire, and I encourage you to seek out such expertise and guidance. This book will be an excellent starting point and ally in your journey, but nothing can fully substitute for professional help.

The Destructive Narcissistic Pattern: Is Your Parent Self-Absorbed?

Self-absorption occurs when there is a continual and extreme focus on one's self in almost every situation and circumstance. Actions by self-absorbed people are based on their needs most or all of the time, even when some of their acts seem to benefit others. This book presents this continual and extreme self-focus as a Destructive Narcissistic Pattern (DNP) (Brown 1998, 2001, 2006).

Following are the behaviors and attitudes that tend to indicate a DNP. Read the descriptions to determine which fits your parent. It is not necessary that the parent have or demonstrate all of these traits, as long as they have many of them and they are troubling to your relationship with the parent.

Grandiosity: Your parent has unreasonable expectations for success, performance, wealth, and the like. The parent wants to win all of the time, knows what's best for others, and does not have a logical or reasonable sense of their personal limitations.

Entitlement attitude: This attitude is one that assumes that everyone else is just an extension of one's self and therefore that others are under one's control and just exist to meet one's own needs, even unspoken ones. Others are not recognized as separate and distinct individuals. The parent expects and demands preferential treatment and feels that their needs should receive priority over the needs of others.

Lack of empathy: The parent is indifferent to the impact of their critical, demeaning, and devaluing comments about you and others, but simultaneously expects others to be empathic toward the parent. The parent constantly blames others for mistakes and for what cannot be changed.

Extensions of self: Since the parent does not recognize others as separate individuals, the parent expects favors but does not return them. The parent gives orders and expects these to be promptly carried out, and expects others to know what is wanted without the parent having to speak. The parent asks intrusive personal questions and tells others what they should or ought to do, and doesn't respect others' property or boundaries.

Impoverished self: The behaviors that signal the impoverished self include constantly complaining about being deprived, excluded, or minimized, even when there is no evidence to support this perspective. The parent may be self-depreciating, but will become angry or hurt if others agree with the self-depreciating comments. The self-absorbed parent will use personal put-downs in an effort to get others to disagree.

Attention seeking: Most of these behaviors and attitudes are easily seen, as the parent usually does some or all of them. Examples includes speaking loudly, talking a lot, entering and exiting rooms noisily, dressing to attract attention, and making grand gestures.

Admiration seeking: These behaviors are those that are constantly done for public approval and approbation, which the parent craves as external signs of worthiness, superiority, and the like. The parent boasts and brags about their accomplishments and is self-promoting for awards and other recognitions. The parent responds to flattery but does not recognize insincere compliments.

Shallow emotions: Self-absorbed parents express and experience few emotions, usually only anger and fear. They use the words for feelings, but these are empty and meaningless.

Envy: Envy is displayed by saying and doing things that reflect resentment of others' success, accomplishments, possessions, or opportunities. The parent reacts by feeling that other persons are not deserving. Feelings of envy can trigger the impoverished self.

Contempt: Contempt is a part of feeling superior, where the person thinks that others are less deserving, worthwhile, or valuable. An example is when the parent makes negative and demeaning comments about others' value and worth, such as that poor people do not deserve assistance.

Arrogance: This attitude of feeling vastly superior to others can be seen in behaviors such as talking down or patronizingly to others. The parent is not shy about letting others know that they are perceived as inferior and makes frequent references to the parent's own superiority.

Emptiness at the core of self: The empty person perceives relationships as existing for personal convenience and hops from relationship to relationship, never able to make real connections. Such a person is unable to form and maintain meaningful, satisfying, and enduring relationships, becomes very anxious when alone, and seems to crave or need activity.

Reverse parenting: This occurs when the child is made responsible for the parent's well-being instead of the usual expectation that the parent is responsible for the child's well-being. Behaviors that signal this attitude include statements like the following: "If you loved me, you would…" "I love you when you…" "Don't you want me to love you?" "You make me feel good when you…" "I don't like it when you disappoint me." "Can't you ever do what I want or need you to do?"

Basks in the child's reflected glory: This parent demands that the child become and do what the parent desires, for example, by excelling in athletics and school achievement or displaying other talents. The child must be very successful or the parent will be displeased. The parent is also indifferent to or ignores the child's own desires.

Intolerant of child's values and needs: The parent cannot perceive the child as a separate and distinct individual, but only as an extension of the parent. They cannot tolerate disagreement or any hint of criticism, want to always be perceived as perfect, and blame the child for any perceived imperfections and mistakes.

Exploits others: This behavior and attitude are also reflections of an inability to perceive and relate to others as separate, different, and worthwhile individuals. Others are perceived as existing for the parent's benefit and as subject to exploitive behaviors, such as taking unfair advantage of others, manipulating others, and assuming unearned credit.

What you have probably realized from reading these descriptions with your parent in mind, is that your parent had some of these characteristics but not others. But if you believe that your parent has numerous characteristics reflective of self-absorption, then you will want to read further to understand better the impact that had on you as you were developing, as well as the lingering impact on you currently. Later in this chapter you will find descriptions of various types of self-absorbed parents, and your parent's behavior and attitudes may seem to indicate a particular type. But it's important to remember that these descriptions and categories are not definitive. They are used for ease of discussion.

The Child Who Assumed Parental Responsibilities

The self-absorbed parents described here have many of the characteristics described above, and in addition have a conscious or unconscious expectation that their children are responsible for their parents' welfare instead of the reverse. Children growing up under these circumstances experience all or most of the following:

- The adult child still exists as an extension of the parent.

- The child remains under parental control even after becoming an adult.

- The child must meet parental expectations at all times, even as an adult with their own needs and self-expectations.

- The child must be able to anticipate parental needs and desires and work diligently to fulfill them.

- The child must attend to and at all times admire the parent.

- The child is expected to sacrifice their life and welfare to take care of the parent.

- The child must show empathy to the parent but not expect or receive empathy in return.

- The child must never make mistakes or show poor judgment, as this would reflect negatively on the parent.

- The child is expected to drop what they are doing at any moment if the parent wants them to.

- The child must never exercise any independence or autonomy.

The children of self-absorbed parents, who experience these behaviors and attitudes from birth, are not allowed to become separate and distinct individuals in their own right, and may find that this affects their adult lives in often negative ways. Read the following and assess if the thought, feeling, or attitude fits you today:

- Do you have difficulty forming satisfying and meaningful relationships that endure?

- Are you unable to recognize when others are trying to manipulate you to do things that are not in your best interests?

- Do you find it difficult to express a wide variety of emotions?

- Do you become overwhelmed by others' emotions and find it hard to let go of them?

- Do you become enmeshed in others' emotions?

- Do you tend to take others' comments and actions personally?

- Do you have difficulty controlling negative feelings such as anger and resentment?

- Do you stay on edge and anxious about trying to please others?

- Do you have difficulty making decisions for fear of making mistakes?

- Do you wonder why others seem to find more happiness and pleasure than you do?

If you resonated with many of these, then you may have enduring negative effects that have their roots in having grown up with a destructive, narcissistic parent. It could be that your current actions, feelings, and relationships are reflective of how you were expected to act and relate with your self-absorbed parent.

Effects of Reverse Parenting

Following are descriptions of how reverse parenting may affect the emotional susceptibility of the adult child. As you read these, try to rate how often or intensely you experience what is described.

One of the most troubling and enduring effects of reverse parenting can be heightened emotional susceptibility. Emotional susceptibility is the tendency to "catch" others' feelings (usually negative feelings), incorporate these feelings into your self, and then find that you are unable to easily release them. Your psychological boundary strength was not sufficiently developed as you were growing up, so you're less able to screen out and choose which emotions of others you can accept and which the other person should keep. Do you find that you do any or all of the following?

- Constantly monitor others and try to discern what they are feeling, so that you can take care of them if they seem to need something or to be in distress.

- Become upset when others are in distress and find it difficult to let go of those feelings.

- Feel that you must have others' liking and approval most or all of the time.

- Take on the responsibility for others' welfare or emotional well-being, even if they are independent adults who can care for themselves.

- Stay constantly on edge, churned up, or even upset, and cannot let go of these feelings.

- Feel fearful of any signals that there is conflict present, even when you are not involved.

- Feel positive or happy only when those around you are feeling the same way.

If you found that many of these descriptions fit you, then the following discussion may provide you with some understanding of what may be happening. Your emotional susceptibility and psychological boundary strength may be contributing to some of your more distressing feelings.

Two Responses to a Parental DNP

There are two major responses children seem to have when their parent has a DNP: compliance or rebellion. The compliant response has the child trying harder and harder to please the parent, a reaction that extends into adulthood, where considerable effort goes into trying to always please others and anxiety is experienced when others do not seem to be pleased. This response also includes searching anxiously for nonverbal signals of distress, desires, or needs; the inability to be content with less than perfection; never feeling adequate; and relying mostly on others for validation.

The rebellious response occurs when the child does not try to please the parent because they realize that pleasing the parent is not possible. The child then acts in a way that conveys that they don't care what others think about them. They don't try to discern what others want or need, keep a distance from others, and retreat into a self-protective stance. This stance makes it difficult for this person to trust others and works against establishing meaningful and satisfying relationships.

Types of Self-Absorbed Parents

There are many self-absorbed behaviors and attitudes, and it can be confusing when your parent has some but not others. For ease of discussion, we can categorize four types of self-absorbed parents: needy, prickly, conniving, and grandstanding. Each will be presented, with a basic description, a list of behaviors, and the possible responses of the compliant child and the rebellious child.

Needy: The needy self-absorbed parent can come across to others as very caring and concerned. This parent is usually attentive, tries to anticipate every need, and is very anxious about getting recognition for their efforts. This need for recognition, specifically, is very suggestive of self-absorption. This parent has to receive attention, appreciation, and approval for almost every parental act, both from the child and from others. The child is not cared for altruistically—the child is expected to "pay" for the care with emotional coin. Any suggestion that the parent's efforts are not wanted or appreciated, such as a toddler exerting their burgeoning independence, can result in the parent's displeasure or in the parent's taking control and managing the child (for example, by overprotecting). This parent makes sure others know how hard they work, sacrifice, and care, so that no one can ever overlook or forget about it.

Behaviors and attitudes reflective of the needy self-absorbed parent are clinging, overnurturing, and a tendency to be overprotective. Such parents may make a big deal out of what they think of as their personal sacrifices, complain a lot about a lot of things, and seem to get anxious when they are alone. They pester you to know your every thought, feeling, and idea, never forget an offense, and can be easily hurt since they are hypersensitive to perceived criticism. Such parents are never empathic, but they may appear to be sympathic.

Prickly: Prickly self-absorbed parents are very demanding and expect prompt and accurate compliance with their needs, whether or not these needs have been verbally conveyed. Others are expected to "do the right thing," to always "do it right," without ever receiving an adequate explanation of what "right" means for the parent. This parent can also be very touchy, sensing disapproval, criticism, and blame from almost everything that is said and done, whether or not that is what was actually meant. As a consequence, the child is always tense around this type of parent, careful in what they say and do, and continues to try to "get it right" or to withdraw physically or emotionally.

Some behaviors and attitudes these parents display are never being completely satisfied, being very critical of others, and being picky so that everything must be done as the parent wants and must be up to the parent's standards. Such parents demand perfection, blame the child and others for their discomfort, make demeaning or devaluing comments to and about the child and others, and take offense easily at what the parent takes as criticism.

Conniving: Conniving self-absorbed parents are always positioning themselves to win, to come out on top, to be superior to others, and to make sure that all others understand that they are inferior. This applies to almost all aspects of their life, including their children. Such parents will lie, cheat, distort, and mislead in order to achieve their goals. Others are considered fair game for manipulation and exploitation, including their children. Such parents can be adept at reading others' needs and emotional susceptibilities and using this knowledge to manipulate and exploit others. Some effects on their children when they become adults are a wariness and constant questioning of others' motives or a tendency to get into relationships where they are manipulated to do things they do not want to do or that aren't in their best interest.

Behaviors and attitudes reflective of the conniving parent include being manipulative, having a must-win-at-any-cost perspective, and having a willingness to lie, cheat, mislead, and distort to get what is wanted—sometimes just to see if others will be conned. Such parents may be coercive, seductive, and ingratiating to get what they want. They take advantage of others, are dismissive of others as being inferior to them, are vengeful, and are always looking for the main chance or an edge over everyone else. This type of parent assumes that others are supposed to do what the parent wants without questioning, and that others are just like them, so they have to get their licks in first.

Grandstanding: The grandstanding parent can be described as "always on stage," "playing to the crowd," and "larger than life." Others in this parent's world have to assume a subordinate role, and that role must support and highlight the parent's self-perception. This parent's children are perceived as extensions of the parent, and the children exist to enhance and expand the areas where the parent can be admired, receive attention, be better than others, and so on. The child must never fail; and when the child succeeds, that success is perceived as due to the parent's efforts or contributions. The effects on these children can produce someone who is timid, cautious, and always seeking attention and admiration, or someone who acts out to get the same outcomes as does the parent.

Some characteristic behaviors and attitudes for this type of self-absorbed parent include being flamboyant and dramatic, constantly boasting and bragging, and exaggerating their accomplishments and even their ailments. Such parents are very restless, moving from relationship to relationship, from project to project, and seem to always be moving to the next thing. They engage in considerable self-promotion, overestimate their personal abilities, capabilities, and talents, and resent others who get the spotlight for better performance. They can also be very intrusive and dismissive of others' psychological boundaries, possessions, or personal space, and assume charge of just about everything.

Responses to the Self-Absorbed Parental Types

There are two categories of responses the children of self-absorbed parents can employ to try and protect themselves from the more destructive aspects of their parent: *compliance* and *rebellion*. Now we'll show how each of these types of response can react to the four types of self-absorbed parents.

Responses to the Needy Parent

Compliant response: Compliant children who have a needy self-absorbed parent may, even as adults, be overly sensitive to others' needs. Some of their unconscious responses can be constantly monitoring others for signs of distress; trying to discern others' unmet needs; and trying to read other people's minds, attempting to know how to respond or behave even before a request is made. Such adult children are still very anxious and fearful of disagreements and other forms of conflict, will subordinate their own personal needs most of the time, feel guilt and shame when others are disappointed, and do things that they don't want to do in an effort to please others. In so doing, they can be easily seduced and often become enmeshed in others' feelings.

Rebellious response: Children who respond rebelliously to the behavior of the needy narcissistic parent as adults will tend to keep others at a distance, often refusing to connect or engage. These adult children of self-absorbed parents may be insensitive or may ignore others' needs. They tend to openly disagree with others, but then withdraw from conflict. They are resentful when others try to seduce or coerce them.

Responses to the Prickly Parent

Compliant response: Children with a prickly self-absorbed parent who tend to have a compliant response will, as adults, try hard to please and can be fearful of conflict. When they become an adult, they tend to be perfectionists, but they feel like imposters for their achievements and are unable to accept or believe compliments. As both children and adults, they cringe at the slightest hint of criticism or blame, are susceptible to being bullied, and try to discern what is expected and comply.

Rebellious response: Children who respond rebelliously to a prickly parent are defiant, tend to be combative, and are overly defensive in response to comments perceived as critical, and this behavior continues into adulthood. They use attack as a first defense, are not concerned with pleasing others, and do not recognize or accept support from others.

Responses to the Conniving Parent

Compliant response: The compliant responder to a conniving self-absorbed parent will have a façade of the false self that is also presented when the child becomes an adult, being overly complimentary and ingratiating, but also sneaky and loose with the truth. This person can be easily seduced or coerced, is fearful of being rejected, and is anxious and never confident about what to expect.

Rebellious response: Children who respond rebelliously to a conniving self-absorbed parent are wary of others and tend to mistrust others' motives. They may be hard to get to know, because they fear that other people are trying to coerce or seduce them. They think that others are trying to take advantage of them and are constantly on guard for others' hidden agendas.

Responses to the Grandstanding Parent

Compliant response: Children who respond compliantly to a grandstanding self-absorbed parent will tend to be submissive, self-effacing, and self-deprecating. They will always be on edge, trying to anticipate the unexpected, fearing and expecting the worst, and they are unable to protect personal psychological boundaries.

Rebellious response: Children who respond rebelliously to a grandstanding self-absorbed parent tend to engage in risky behavior that can be self-destructive. They use flattery as a tool and may appear cooperative, but they often have quiet or hidden defiance and have considerable resistance to others' ideas, while being adept at concealing their true feelings.

Summary and Next Steps

At this point, you have some indications of whether or not your parent has many of the behaviors and attitudes of the DNP, and have identified your primary response as either compliant or rebellious. There can be some overlapping of categories, types, and responses, but the types are only provided for ease of discussion and you can make adjustments to what is presented to fit you and your situation.

The material in the rest of this book is intended to guide you to a better understanding of how you developed and grew to become the person you are at this time, to teach you strategies that can be helpful when interacting with your self-absorbed parent, and to show you how to lessen or eliminate the negative impact of that parent's behavior and attitudes on you. Among the gains you may experience are:

- Learning a process for containing and managing your difficult feelings so that you resist manipulation, seduction, and coercion, especially by your parent.

- Becoming more realistic about your parent and relinquishing the fantasy that the parent will change and become the parent you long for.

- Discovering what to do and say in interactions with the parent—including actions that can prevent your negative feelings from being aroused.

- Building your capacity for empathy, creativity, and other characteristics of healthy adult narcissism so that you can be the person you want to be.

- Reducing your faulty beliefs and your undeveloped narcissism so as to have better relationships, meaning, and purpose for your life, and find inner satisfaction.

- Overcoming many of the lingering effects produced by living with a parent with a DNP.

- Learning strategies for how to handle difficult situations with the parent, especially when others are present.

- Gaining the freedom to become the person you want to be, unencumbered or less encumbered by lingering effects of your self-absorbed parent.

CHAPTER ACTIVITIES

Visualization

(If you want to draw what emerges, gather drawing materials in advance: one or more sheets of paper and a set of crayons, felt markers, or colored pencils.)

Sit in silence, close your eyes (or if that makes you uncomfortable, leave your eyes open) and allow a scene of peace where you can be calm to emerge. You can also stop the visualization at any time by opening your eyes. As you visualize this scene, try to note as many details as possible: sounds, scents, colors, and so on. Notice how you feel as you are visualizing and how the scene evolves. When you are ready, open your eyes and draw the scene if you like. (That may help to fix the scene in your mind.) You can return to this peaceful calm place at any time just by thinking about it and allowing it to emerge. Use this scene when you become distressed by the thoughts, feelings, and other reactions that emerge as you think about your parent.

Writing

Find a place to work where you will not be disturbed or interrupted and have readily available a sheet of paper and a writing instrument. Write a description of your parent as you see the parent today. Note any of the self-absorbed behaviors and attitudes listed in this chapter.

Drawing/Collage

Gather the materials for drawing or for a collage. Draw or collage five or six symbols of yourself as you are today. Focus on what you consider to be the most basic or significant aspects of yourself for the symbols—for example, a sun for your spirits.

CHAPTER 2

Lingering Effects of Parental Self-Absorption

Gary was forty-five years old, was married, and had a very demanding and responsible job where he was productive and well paid. He was liked and approved of by his wife and children and colleagues at work, and seemed to have a meaningful and productive life. However, Gary constantly questioned his competency, adequacy, and likeability, and could be easily manipulated at times. He kept trying to please others, sometimes to his personal discomfort and distress. He did not see why he could not say no and stick to it, was constantly seeking others' approval, and was always striving to achieve some fantasized level of competency which he could not explain or describe.

How Early Experiences Can Affect the Child as an Adult

Some parental actions and messages that happened early in the child's life can still be affecting the child as an adult. These actions and messages were powerful, incorporated by the child without the child knowing or realizing what was happening. They became a part of the child's self-esteem, and are still exerting effects on the child as an adult, some of which may be unconscious. The negative effects of these parental actions and messages produced deep hurts during childhood, and those wounds have not yet healed. What follows is an explanation of how some early parental messages and actions may still be affecting them as an adult, and the role these early hurts play in the adult's self-perception.

Narcissistic Wounding

Narcissistic wounds are injuries to the essential self of the person. These wounds are produced by the messages a person receives that suggest that the person is fatally flawed, not valued, has little worth, and so on. Wounding may occur early in life before the child has the words to express the self-thoughts, feelings, and ideas that are internalized from the messages that were received. Because the parents are usually the people who take care of the child, even the way a parent handles and responds to the infant or child can send a message about how the parent perceives the child. When the infant or child is not responded to in a positive way, this can produce narcissistic wounding that lingers. That initial wound can be reinforced by other wounding, and the cumulative effect is a negative perception of oneself as an adult.

You, of course, did not recognize what was happening at the time and may not yet be fully aware of how your childhood experiences continue to affect your adult self, your relationships, and some of your actions. Your parent's responses to you, their conscious and unconscious messages to you about your essential inner self, and your personality and responses to your parent—all these interacted to produce the injuries and lack of development you are probably dealing with today.

The parent's response to you as a developing child carried considerable importance for your self-esteem. Parental empathic attunement and response helps build a child's self-esteem. If your parent was unable or unwilling to provide sufficient empathy because of their self-absorption, then you did not receive the empathy conducive to feeling worthy, cherished, and loved. While not all of your self-esteem is affected by empathy or its lack, you may still be struggling with major self-esteem deficits.

Parental conscious and unconscious messages are also received by the child consciously and unconsciously, incorporated into the self, and acted on, usually in nonconscious ways. That is, you are not aware of how these messages are affecting your thoughts and feelings about your essential inner self, your attitudes and responses to and about others, and your actions. These parental messages are powerful influences. You received messages about how your parent perceived your value as a person, your looks, your intelligence and abilities, your role in the family, expectations for what you were to be and do, how much you were loved, and other such messages. It's not hard to understand the importance and the continuing effects of parental messages.

Each person is different, and each has a unique personality and response to their parents. These interact and produce results unique to each person, although some can be generalized. That is, everyone with a self-absorbed parent can have injuries to the self that linger as the child becomes an adult, but different people are injured in different ways. In this chapter, we'll be looking at some possible effects of consciously and unconsciously internalized parental messages on adult children of self-absorbed parents.

Did You Suffer Early Narcissistic Wounding?

How can you begin to understand how you are narcissistically wounded when you suffered an injury to your essential self that has not healed? If the injury happened when you were an infant or a toddler, it may have been forgotten, since it happened before you developed the capacity to store memories in the language you use and understand today. These early injuries can nevertheless still impact you in indirect, hidden, and masked ways. For example, some will find that they cannot initiate and maintain meaningful and enduring relationships, and others will find that they are easily wounded by criticism. Early wounding carries over to today, lurks and affects you in unconscious ways, negatively affects your self-esteem, and can result in self-destructive behaviors.

It is important that you understand yourself and any beliefs about your worth and value you may have that are a result of your early wounding. For example, do you have a belief that you must have intimate and close relationships in order to feel loved, competent, worthwhile, safe, and valued? Do you find that you enter less than satisfying relationships trying to find the person who can give you the love you are yearning for? If so, then you will want to consider how your current actions may be the result of your deep-seated needs that came from the deficient parenting you received from your self-absorbed parent.

Signals of Possible Early Parental Narcissistic Wounding

Here are some indicators that signal narcissistic wounding. Read the following self-statements and reflect if this is a thought or feeling that you have frequently with many people, or that is triggered in some interactions where you experience distress.

- I am very flawed, and if others can see my flaws, they will not like or approve of me.

- I am not living up to my values and principles, because I let others manipulate me.

- I am unable to protect myself from doing what others want me to do.

- I think that most other people are more competent, capable, and adequate than I am.

- I live in fear that I am in danger of being seen as I really am and that I will be destroyed when this happens.

- I cannot survive if others don't like and approve of me.

- I cannot prevent others from destroying or abandoning me.

How true do these self-statements feel as you read them? Other signals can include the following:

- You have personal relationships that are unstable or unhealthy.

- You have considerable dissatisfaction with yourself, such as with your appearance.

- You never or seldom feel satisfied or that you have enough.

- You never feel good enough.

- You are never able to trust others.

- You lack meaning or purpose for your life.

- You constantly make negative self-statements.

If you resonate with two or more of these statements, then you may have experienced early narcissistic wounding. Below are some suggestions for how you can understand the impact of this early wounding on you today, and some steps you can take to begin to heal.

Beliefs About Your Self

Self-statements such as those previously listed can be illogical and irrational thoughts you have about yourself that allow you to be wounded. These will be discussed in this chapter, and I will suggest substitute self-statements that are more reasonable and rational.

You become injured because of your beliefs about your essential inner self that lead to the negative self-statements, not because of what someone else says or does. If you did not have these beliefs about your essential inner self, then what others said or did would not produce these negative feelings. Some beliefs are conscious ones, and you are aware of them. Others may be suppressed just below the level of awareness but can emerge at any time, while others are buried deep in your unconscious, and the only way you have any hint that they exist is through your reactions. You may consciously deny that you have these beliefs about yourself, but you would not have these negative feelings if you did not have some versions of these self-beliefs. Your challenge is to begin to know and understand your beliefs about yourself and to work to change those that are negative, defeating, and not constructive.

Self-statements that may be contributing to your injuries can include the following:

I must have others' approval to survive. It feels supportive and encouraging when others approve of you. You can be confident that you are accepted and will not be abandoned or destroyed when you have their approval. While this may appear to be somewhat extreme as presented here, the fear that underlies the need for approval is very basic, even though it's usually not expressed as fear. Everyone has some fear of being abandoned or destroyed, and everyone wants approval.

If you received sufficient approval from family and other significant people in your early life environment, you probably developed enough self-confidence to believe that you are acceptable, and that others will be supportive and encouraging. Sufficient basic approval means that someone liked and accepted you as you were.

I have an obligation to be perfect. The belief that you have an obligation to be perfect can cause you much distress, as you can never be fully satisfied with your essential inner self. You never seem to quite reach perfection, and no external reassurance that you are good enough is sufficient to help you like or be more accepting of yourself. You may even extend your need to be perfect to others in your world and demand that they, too, be perfect. This extension to others can be detrimental to your relationships.

It is my responsibility to always take care of others. Although it is commendable to be concerned about others, it is not reasonable for you to automatically assume responsibility for everyone, to be overly protective, to not accept and believe that others are capable of self-care, to be intrusive with your acts of caring, to insist that others accept these acts, or to feel guilty or ashamed when others are in distress. These are signs that you may be overly responsible, that you don't understand the limits of your personal responsibility and that you are unaware of others' desires for independence and autonomy. In these cases, you are most likely unconsciously trying to fulfill old parental messages. Thus, when you do not or cannot meet any or all of these demands on you, you become anxious, guilty, or ashamed.

Other people's needs are more important than mine. You may have internalized early in your life that your needs were not as important as others' needs were. Lack of empathy from a parent or caretaker, neglect, blame, criticism, failure to accept you as you are and appreciate your qualities, and other such experiences could have shaped your belief that others' needs should be placed above your own. It will be difficult for you to overcome this belief and achieve a satisfactory balance between appropriate self-care and the need to take care of others.

I am flawed so badly that I cannot ever be better. Despair, hopelessness, and helplessness are apt to emerge when you believe that you are so flawed that you can never get better.

These feelings emerge at times when you are hurt and ashamed and can lead to depression. It can seem that no matter how hard you try, you continue to make the same mistakes or draw the same criticisms, blame, and other demeaning comments. You don't know why you can't "get it right" when other people don't seem to have that problem.

I cannot survive without someone to take care of me. Usually, when people think or feel that they need another person to take care of them, the thought or feeling is about emotional and psychological caretaking. Adults who need physical care are correct in this belief and are not included in this discussion. We are really talking here about needing intimate and close relationships with other people. Having such a belief about yourself can lead you to considerable hurt and to feeling rejected. You can then be vulnerable to entering into destructive relationships, doing things you don't want to do, and tolerating acts that demean and devalue you.

I must not let others see the real me, because they would then reject me. There are aspects of yourself that you know about but want to keep hidden from others, because you fear or expect that they will reject you if they should ever become aware of that part of you. You probably think of that part of your essential inner self as the "real" you. Thus, things others do or say that lead you to believe that they are aware of the real you can be painful because, in your mind, that awareness is most likely to lead to rejection.

I am not as good (capable, intelligent, and so on) as others are. When you think and feel that you are not as good or as adequate as others, this leaves you open to injury and reinjury, because you are constantly faced with evidence that some other people are richer, smarter, more talented, better looking, of higher status, and so on. In addition, every mistake you make becomes more evidence for your negative belief about your essential inner self. Comments and remarks by others that appear to focus on your weaknesses and negative aspects can produce even more validations of your negative beliefs, and these are very wounding. Your self can remain in a constant state of hurt.

I can never get what I want or need. If you think or feel that you can never get what you want or need, you have a belief that you lack self-efficacy. This belief may have been established early in your life, even as an infant, when your self-absorbed parent delayed in attending in your needs, or neglected you, or even showed indifference to you.

Negative Statements and Self-Affirmations

Let's explore these negative and illogical self-statements for their validity, logic, and usefulness, and consider some self-affirmations that can help counter them.

••• **Negative statement:** *I require others' approval.*

If your experiences with your parent were such that you received approval only for things like the following, then you may not think consciously or unconsciously that you receive sufficient approval:

- You always had to fully meet your parent's needs.

- You were expected to read your parent's mind and anticipate what the parent wanted or needed.

- The parent only told you they were pleased when you did something for the parent, but not just for being who you are.

- You had major accomplishments that were a source of pride for the parent, and the parent took pleasure in boasting, bragging, and other ways of showing their approval of you.

- You received parental approval only or mostly when you won, came out on top, or were successful.

Self-affirmation: *I like and want this person's approval, but I will be okay if I don't get it.*

···

··· **Negative statement:** *I must be perfect.*

How did this belief come about? When did you internalize and become convinced that the only way to survive was to be perfect? Notice that this belief is not striving for perfection—it is a belief that you must *be* perfect. Even when you rationally know that perfection is not needed and cannot be attained, you cannot let go of your belief that you must be perfect. Your early experiences of parental criticisms and lack of parental empathy for your errors and mistakes contributed to this belief.

What could be helpful is for you to realize that your focus on perfection is not constructive for you or for your relationships. You can act on this realization by working to become more satisfied with being good enough while still striving to be and do better. You can be perfect in some ways but still accepting of yourself and others as less than perfect in other ways. This will enable you to be less easily injured when you don't meet your expectations for perfection and when you don't meet others' expectations. Practice the following self-affirmation, because believing this can also lead you to become more accepting of the flaws in others.

Self-affirmation: *Being good enough is sufficient. I will work to be better, but I still like myself even when I am not perfect.*

···

••• **Negative statement:** *I need to take care of others.*

The key to this characteristic is the extent to which you think and feel that it is your responsibility to take care of others. It's reasonable for you to assume this responsibility for those who need this care, such as children or the elderly, or when such care is your job or profession, and it's perfectly okay to have care and concern for those who are less fortunate and in distress.

How does feeling overly responsible for others' welfare contribute to your injury or reinjury? I've already presented one way—you feel guilty and ashamed when others experience discomfort or distress, and that opens you up to feeling less positive about yourself. There are other situations that can produce guilt and shame, such as when a friend or relative tells you to butt out of their business and that you are being intrusive.

You will want to keep the caring and helpful part of this and let go of the part that pushes you to always be the lead, front-and-center person and director of helpfulness. Learn when this is your responsibility and accept when it is not. Try the following self-affirmation before you rush to offer your help.

Self-affirmation: *I may help more by showing confidence that the other person can fix it.*

•••

••• **Negative statement:** *I must see to others' needs.*

Another belief that is closely associated with the previous one is a notion that others' needs are more important than yours are. There are times and circumstances where this is the case and you must subordinate your needs for those of someone else. For example, you may need to subordinate your needs if someone you love is ill, if you're caring for children or the elderly, and sometimes if this is part of your job. I'm not talking about situations such as these. I am talking about a mindset that does not allow you to ever put your needs ahead of anyone else's.

Whenever you feel the need to take care of others before your needs get met, ask yourself, "Will the person or the relationship really suffer if I attend to my needs?" If the answer is that you would not feel right if you took care of your needs first, or that you would feel better if you put their needs first, then use the following self-affirmation.

Self-affirmation: *I deserve to be given preference sometimes, and self-care is also important.*

...

··· **Negative statement:** *I am badly flawed.*

In addition to the hurt caused by external events, you can incur even more pain from your beliefs about your essential inner self. You may even feel, on some level, that you have many more flaws than do other people, although if someone were to ask if you thought this, you would probably deny it. You're hoping that others don't perceive you as you perceive yourself, although you really fear that they do. You probably use a variety of attitudes, defenses, and other strategies to cover up your feelings and self-perceptions, such as arrogance, rationalization, or denial.

You don't feel good about yourself, but you don't want others to know this because you fear that they would abandon or destroy you. This leaves you vulnerable to injury and reinjury, where the hurt self is subjected to even more pain. This happens many times over the years until it really doesn't take much at all to injure you.

Overcoming your negative self-perception and building a more positive one will take considerable time and effort, and I encourage you to get started right away. Until you've worked more, either alone or with assistance, try the following self-affirmation whenever you feel ashamed, hopeless, or helpless.

Self-affirmation: *I can do better and I will.*

...

••• **Negative statement:** *I need someone to take care of me.*

You will do almost anything to keep from being alone, but seem to derive little joy or satisfaction from your relationships. Even in a relationship, you feel alone. For the time being, try the following self-affirmation every day for the next month, or however long you wish.

Self-affirmation: *I am strong enough to survive on my own. I can build constructive and satisfying relationships.*

•••

••• **Negative statement:** *I can't reveal the real me.*

The real you may be hidden even from yourself. Everyone has aspects of their self that they do not see but others do, and also aspects that are inaccessible for one reason or another. Uncovering our real selves can be a lifelong task and may need the assistance of a competent mental health professional. Whatever the reasons for hiding your real self, you can still be injured, because you cannot fully hide everything you want to keep hidden. Yes, there are people who seem to be able to do this. But a careful examination of their situations and circumstances is likely to reveal that others have, in fact, seen some of these supposedly shameful aspects but the wounded person refuses to consciously acknowledge that they were seen. Such persons use denial, repression, or considerable rationalization to explain away what the other person saw or sensed.

You may want to explore for yourself the personal characteristics you want to keep hidden and why it is important to you to put on a façade. This doesn't mean that you need to reveal all your secrets or to be constantly telling others about characteristics that you perceive as less than desirable. You don't have to do either of these. It helps to simply be aware that you do have secrets and characteristics that you prefer to keep hidden for fear that others will reject you.

Self-affirmation: *I can let more of my real self be revealed to others and, as I like parts of my essential inner self better, I can let more of my real self be seen by others.*

...

... **Negative statement:** *I am helpless to make changes.*

Have you tried to change something but were unsuccessful? If you're like most people, you have tried to change and became frustrated when there was no payoff, what you did was not entirely successful, or what you did even seemed to make the situation worse. You may have repeatedly tried to make changes, only to be unsuccessful. This can be especially shaming when what you were trying to change was a personal characteristic, whether it was one that you wanted to change or one that someone else wanted you to change.

What do you want to change about yourself, and why do you want these changes? What gets in the way of your being success-ful in making these changes? You are not helpless to make changes, although you may not have been successful in the past. You just haven't yet found what you need to do and how to do it. But, on some level, you may have convinced yourself that you are unable to do so because you are essentially flawed. This feeling of being flawed is what you find to be shaming and what continues to contribute to your feeling helpless.

Change involves several steps, beginning with understand-ing what you are experiencing. The next steps are to think through why you're reacting as you are, develop a plan for making changes one step at a time, and give yourself permis-sion to not be entirely successful all at once. Some changes may need expert help, and that too can reduce your feeling of helplessness. Try this self-affirmation when you feel helpless about making personal changes:

Self-affirmation: *I can change, but I have not yet found a way to do it. I will not give up.*

···

··· **Negative statement:** *I'm not as worthwhile as others.*

Other terms for thinking and feeling that you are not as worthwhile as others include low self-esteem, lack of self-confidence, and feelings of inferiority. Such terms point to a personal perception of one's self that is unfavorable when compared to other people. This perception also includes an unrealistic expectation that you are not worthy unless you are as good as or superior to others in every way. What is more realistic, and can lead to better self-acceptance, is the realization and acceptance that you have some strengths and some weaknesses. You have aspects of your essential inner self that need work or development—and others do, too. You are not in a contest, there will not be winners and losers, and you are not helping yourself when you focus on these kinds of comparisons.

You may find it helpful to focus more on your strengths. Don't ignore or deny your weaknesses and what needs developing; continue to work on these, but try to get in the habit of not dwelling on them, as that can make them seem worse than they really are and does nothing that helps you overcome them. Overall, you are as worthwhile and valuable as other people, even with your flaws and faults. Try the following self-affirmation:

Self-affirmation: *Most mistakes can be corrected. I will do better next time. I need to work on this, but that doesn't make me less worthwhile. I will make the most out of who I am, what I have, and what I am able to do.*

···

••• **Negative statement:** *I can't get what I want or need.*

Think about it. There are very few, if any, adults who cannot take care of most of their needs and wants, especially the basic needs. What this belief about getting your needs met is proposing is that you cannot get others to take care of you, not that your needs and wants are not being met. The finger of blame is pointed at someone else, as if another person should be responsible for meeting your wants and needs. This expectation is reasonable for infants, children, and incapacitated adults, but is not reasonable for most functioning adults. You are responsible for meeting your needs and wants, not other people. Your unrealistic expectations or yearnings are helping to reinjure you every time you have evidence that others will not give you what you want or need.

Self-affirmation: *I can take care of getting most of my needs and wants met for myself.*

•••

Helping Yourself

You now have some suggestions about how you may be opening yourself to injury. In other words, you don't have to hurt as much as you do, you don't have to let what others say and do become criticism and blame, your self can be secure and strong enough to be self-reflective but not shamed by everything, and you don't have to retain hurts, resentments, aggressive thoughts, and self-defeating beliefs. You can develop and fortify your essential inner self so that you have a greater sense of confidence, self-esteem, and self-efficacy. That development has begun if you have increased your awareness of some of your self-defeating behaviors and attitudes, and if you have tried some of the self-affirmations presented in this chapter.

There are some perceptual shifts you can make that will also help. This means that you change your current perception from one that may be self-defeating to another that is more constructive, logical, and realistic. You are not giving up the good parts of yourself when you make these perceptual shifts— you are helping these parts to be stronger and more helpful while at the same time reducing your shame, guilt, fears, sense of inadequacy, and other negative thoughts about yourself. Read each proposed perceptual shift carefully and reflect on your capacity to make the shift.

Shift from:	To:
The need for others' approval	Self-approval
The need for perfection	Satisfaction with being good enough
Overly responsible	Adopting reasonable and limited personal responsibility
Feeling inferior to others	Recognition and acceptance of personal strengths
Dependence	Independence, interdependence, and mutual caring
Lack of self-acceptance	Embracing all parts of your essential inner self, even parts you don't like and want to change
Helplessness, hopelessness	Doing what you can and letting go of the rest

Build a Healthier Core Self

The first part of the chapter provided some suggestions for how your current thoughts, attitudes, and behaviors could be the results of early experiences with your self-absorbed parent and how these may be negatively affecting your self-esteem, self-perception, and even your relationships. Subsequent chapters describe additional suggestions for how to better understand yourself and others, and how to build a healthier core self. While your core self may have many healthy aspects, it is likely that you are not completely satisfied that you are the person you want to be. Your early experiences will likely continue to affect you in conscious and unconscious ways, and better understanding of how these are impacting you today will assist you to overcome some of the negative effects of your self-absorbed parent's behaviors and attitudes.

The most positive thing you can do for yourself is to work to become more of the person that you want to be, so that your essential inner self is confident, effective, and adequate. To this end you will want to work on establishing or increasing the effectiveness of the following characteristics:

Meaning and purpose. Have meaning and purpose for your life, your work, and your relationships. While the meanings and purposes may change throughout your life, it is important that there always be meaning and purpose. Some of the "Chapter Activities" at the end of chapters can assist and guide you in understanding or establishing your meaning and purpose.

Show kindness. Show everyday kindness and altruism. Altruism is the giving of yourself to others without any expectation of reciprocity or reward. It is unselfish giving to others. Everyday kindness is a form of altruism and is helpful for others as well as for yourself.

Become more empathic. Work to become better at empathic responding and relating. Deep empathy is when you are able to enter the world of other persons and sense what they are feeling without losing the sense of yourself as being separate and distinct. You are neither enmeshed with the other people nor overwhelmed by their feelings. However, it is possible to provide empathic responses without using deep empathy. That calls for being able to tune into the other person, identify what the person is feeling without necessarily feeling it yourself, and then verbalizing that feeling to the person. Recognizing and acknowledging others' feelings is very helpful and enriching for relationships.

Build hardiness and resilience. Establish your hardiness and resilience. This doesn't mean that you don't experience or react to adversity; the point is that you don't give in to it. You are down for the time being, but you get back up and either try harder or go in another direction.

Manage your emotions. Manage your difficult emotions, especially those that emerge when in interactions with your self-absorbed parent. Specific instructions and activities for learning how to manage these emotions both in the moment and for the longer term are included in several chapters. When you are able to manage and contain your difficult and sometimes intense emotions, you will be more effective with your self-absorbed parent and with other people, as well as not suffering the lingering effects of these difficult emotions.

Forgive yourself. Learn to forgive yourself when you make mistakes and errors instead of blaming yourself for not being perfect or better. Old parental messages about you contribute to your self-blame, feeling shame and guilt, and other negative thoughts and feelings about yourself. The discussions and activities in this book can guide you to a better understanding of how you can forgive yourself and let go of those negative thoughts and feelings and substitute more sustaining and rewarding ones. This is not to say that you should not work to eliminate or reduce mistakes, but it is better if you don't obsess and blame yourself for them and thereby erode your self-esteem.

These are some elements of a healthy core self that are essential for growing, developing, and healing. In addition, achieving some measure of these elements will enable you to better manage your feelings in interactions with your self-absorbed parent.

CHAPTER ACTIVITIES

Collage: Symbols for My Self

Materials: Five unlined index cards, scissors, crayons or markers, magazines with images, and glue or double-sided tape.

Find a suitable place to work, and use the materials to construct a collage for each of the following aspects of yourself: your cognitive self, your emotional self, your relational self, your creative self, and your inspirational self.

Writing

Write a description of your ideal self, the person you want to be. Be sure to address your ideal cognitive, emotional, relational, physical, inspirational, and creative aspects of yourself.

Visualizing

Visualize your ideal self in your important relationships, and in interactions with your parent. Notice details of how you look, speak, and act, and how that makes you feel.

CHAPTER 3

Still Hurting:
The Child as an Adult

Monica was furious that her mother had called her ungrateful because Monica did not want to go on a vacation with her. Monica was married with two children and a demanding job. She tried to explain to her mother that she could not drop everything to go on a vacation. Her mother did not understand why Monica did not make her mother's desires her first priority. Not only was this happening now, similar things happened almost on a daily basis. Monica tried to not feel guilty when she had to reject her mother's demands, but was unsuccessful as her mother always seemed to play the guilt card and remind Monica of just how much her mother had sacrificed for her. Although Monica tried to maintain a balance between the demands of her adult life, family, and job, she was not always successful, which caused her additional distress.

Injuries to the developing self of the child inflicted in childhood can continue to exert negative effects as the child grows and develops into an adult. Some of these negative effects from childhood can be seen indirectly in the adult's thoughts, feelings, and actions. Many of these injuries are buried in memory that cannot be accessed because they were not stored in a form that is understood after language is developed. This is somewhat like information stored in an early computer language that later computers cannot read because they don't have the old program.

This chapter focuses on identifying and understanding some of the unproductive thoughts and feelings that can be a result of injuries experienced in childhood. We're focusing here on those thoughts and feelings that continue to influence you as an adult and that prevent you from developing a stronger and more cohesive self.

Benefits of This Type of Self-Exploration

It is not always comfortable to engage in self-exploration. Thinking about how you were hurt as a child and recalling those feelings can produce considerable distress. If you start to feel distress, you may want to stop reading for a while and come back to the exploration later. You may also want to use the visualization of the place of peace you developed in chapter 2. However, if you persist even if you are not very comfortable, you can gain numerous benefits for your growth, development, relationships, and life satisfaction.

The benefits of building this stronger essential inner self include the following:

- You develop increased self-confidence and self-esteem and project a more confident you.

- You develop and maintain more meaningful, con- structive, satisfying, and enduring interpersonal relationships.

- You prevent further injury to you by your self-absorbed parent.

- You reduce distressing and negative feelings overall, but most especially in interactions with your parent.

- You become more centered and grounded, feeling more in control of your feelings and actions.

- You have less susceptibility to being reinjured by your parent or by others because of nonconscious or unconscious faulty perceptions about your self.

We'll also begin to examine a process for working with the more intense feelings you have around wounding events from your life. You may think the focus should be on what was done to you and its unfairness, but those wounding events are in the past and there is nothing we can do that will change that past or its impact on you. What we can do is to focus on what you can do to heal yourself, promote positive growth, and achieve a more satisfying self-perception. This approach allows you to take control, to become more effective, and to understand the extent of your personal responsibility for what happens to you, beginning now and for the future.

Overcoming Early Injuries

This section addresses some possible basic assumptions that may unconsciously and negatively affect your current thoughts, reactions, attitudes, and actions. Also presented is a rationale for building a stronger more cohesive essential inner self, how to modify unproductive attitudes and behaviors, and how you may be contributing to further injuries to yourself.

Basic Assumptions

The basic assumptions about what happened to you, and how what happened continues to impact you, include the following:

- Distressing events early in your life, especially those inflicted by your self-absorbed parent, were intensely wounding to your essential self.

- Those past events and relationships continue to impact and influence your self-perception.

- You are unable to release many negative and intense feelings related to these events.

- You cannot go back and change what happened to you.

- Other people, no matter how well-meaning they are or how much they want to help, cannot change the negative feelings you have.

- Apologies from others would not, or did not, lessen the negative feelings you carry.

- Time has not changed your feelings or perceptions of the events or people involved.

- You have a desire to lessen or let go of the negative feelings.

Thus, this process for overcoming early injuries focuses on you and how you can build your essential inner self to be strong, so that you are less vulnerable to becoming reinjured by what your self-absorbed parent says and does, less sensitive to disparaging remarks and actions of others, and less likely to become isolated or alienated. It also asks you to reflect on whether you also unconsciously have some behaviors and attitudes reflective of a Destructive Narcissistic Pattern (DNP) as does your parent.

Build a Strong and Cohesive Self

A strong and cohesive self will permit you to let go of some long-term hurts inflicted by your self-absorbed parent. Even a strong and cohesive self will not prevent you from *ever* being hurt again, but it can make such events happen less often, reduce the intensity of your negative feelings, and allow you to more readily let go of the negativity. This alone is positive for your physical and emotional health and for the quality of your relationships.

A strong and cohesive self will allow you to do all of the following:

- Avoid personalizing what others say and do, because personalizing produces shame, guilt, and additional hurt.

- More accurately judge external threats to yourself and thereby reduce the number of times when you feel anger and fear.

- Understand if and when another person is displacing or projecting what that person finds personally unacceptable onto you, and reject the displacement or projection, enabling you to reduce identifying or acting in accord with the projection.

- More easily let go of minor irritations and annoyances and not let these pile up to where the distress is very uncomfortable.

- Become more accepting of your imperfections and understand that you can change some of them, continue to work on them, and strengthen what you do well.

- Be happier with yourself and with others, which helps you to develop and maintain meaningful and satisfying relationships.

- Be warm, caring, and appropriately empathic with others.

Although a major part of getting rid of old insults, hurts, and the like involves resolving and healing the wounds, the other major part is to further develop your inner self so that you become less susceptible to narcissistic wounding. So that your self is better protected, more firmly grounded, appropriately defended, and not subject to others' assaults or manipulation. So that you become more in charge of what you allow to affect your self.

Modify Unproductive Attitudes and Behaviors

Most everyone has some unproductive attitudes and behaviors that get in the way of developing a healthy and cohesive self. These are the feelings and beliefs about our inner essential selves that erode our self-confidence and self-esteem, and that affect our self-efficacy. These are unproductive because they do not add anything positive to our lives. Read the following list, and reflect on how you may exhibit or experience each trait. As you do so, also reflect on the extent to which the thought or feeling or idea contributes to how you feel about yourself and how that plays into interactions with others.

- You tend to personalize others' comments.

- When something doesn't go right at home or at work, you feel that others are blaming you for what happened.

- You work hard to meet others' expectations and are disappointed in yourself when you fail or don't seem to meet them.

- You feel that other people are pointing out your flaws and imperfections if they don't compliment or praise you.

- It is difficult for you to shrug off or ignore irritations and annoyances.

- You tend to catch other people's feelings, especially their negative feelings, such as anger, disgust, and sadness.

- Your flaws and imperfections are a constant source of shame for you, and you seem to stay very aware of them.

- You believe that it would be helpful if other people were more like you, working on their flaws and imperfections.

- You have continuing questions about the quality of your relationships.

- Although you try to be warm, caring, and empathic with others, you get overwhelmed or enmeshed with their feelings, and that is very uncomfortable.

Now, let's take a look at some key attitudes and behaviors that can tend to undermine the development of a strong, cohesive self. We'll be working on these throughout the book.

Tending to Personalize

Have you ever been told that you are touchy or overly sensitive? Has someone told you that you took a comment as personal when it wasn't meant that way? Does this seem to frequently happen to you? Do you find that much of what others say seems to be pointing a finger of blame or criticism at you? Have you felt this way most or all of your life? If you are answering yes to many of these questions, then you tend to personalize what others say and do.

When you personalize things, you feel that you are being criticized, blamed, and chastised for not being better or for not being good enough. That hurts, especially when coming from loved ones, when you feel it is unfair, or when it is about something over which you have no control or responsibility. Further, when someone tells you to not take it personally, that seems to only add to your distress.

Feeling Blamed

There are many reasons why you may feel that others blame you when things don't go as they had planned, their spoken or unspoken expectations were not met, or they are displeased about something. Some possible reasons you can feel blamed for are the following:

- Others may openly say that you are to blame.

- You may have internalized an old parental message that continues to influence you today.

- One or both parents made you responsible for their psychological or physical welfare, so you are reacting to the new situation as you did with the parent.

- You are a convenient scapegoat to put all of the blame and responsibility on.

- Others find it easier to offload blame, and you are available to take it in.

- You have unrealistic expectations for yourself.

There may be times when you feel blamed even though no one is saying or doing anything that suggests that you are to blame. You take it on yourself and feel awful for whatever it was. You may or may not bear some responsibility for what happened, but you don't bear the entire responsibility; however, that doesn't stop you for taking all the blame.

Taking responsibility for your actions is a very good thing and is a behavior and attitude to be cultivated. However, you may perceive yourself as being blamed when no blame is intended, when you have unrealistic expectations for yourself, or when you don't have a good grasp of the limits of your influence, power, and control.

Then, too, there may be times when you are unfairly being blamed for something, but you still take it in as your responsibility. Others don't want the blame, so they seek ways to make sure they don't get it. You aren't able to defend yourself adequately, so the blame gets loaded onto you. You may even regress some and behave as you did when unfairly blamed by a parent or sibling. This sequence can then lead to other feelings—shame, guilt, and fear.

Disappointing Others and Yourself

If you experience being disappointed in yourself, or feel that you frequently disappoint others, then you may have unrealistic expectations for yourself. Some may be impossible for you to achieve, but in any case there are limits to your personal responsibility for others, especially for those that can care for themselves. Some of your unrealistic expectations for yourself result from the messages received from your self-absorbed parent about how you were expected to take care of the parent. These messages include:

- You are supposed to please others, just as you were expected to please your parent.

- It is your responsibility to see to it that others are not disappointed.

- Other people's needs and desires are more important than yours.

- You become profoundly disappointed in yourself for not being better than you are.

- You tend to assume that others are disappointed without having sufficient evidence that they are, and that you are at fault for not meeting their expectations.

- When someone expresses displeasure or disappointment at just about anything, you assume that person had expectations of you that you failed to meet.

It would be helpful if you could reserve your disappointment in yourself for those times when you actually did fail to live up to your personal standards, ethics, morals, or values. It is also helpful when you vow to not repeat that act again, take steps to understand your behavior, and use your disappointment to make needed changes, instead of beating up on yourself or repressing, denying, or rationalizing what you did. Your basic responsibility is to live up to your own standards; if that pleases others, their approval is icing on the cake. You do not have a responsibility to always please others, nor do you have a responsibility to monitor your actions so that others are not disappointed. You are not responsible for others' feelings, just as others are not responsible for your feelings. Yes, you may do or say something that they view as disappointing, but the choice of what they feel is up to them. The important thing is that you act in accord with your own values, and in a manner so that you will not be disappointed in yourself.

Expecting Compliments and Praise

Are you a person who requires positive feedback and kind words in order to know and feel that you are behaving as expected or meeting others' approval, or that others like you? Is it wounding when you don't get these? Do you then feel that you weren't good enough or you would have been complimented and praised? Receiving some acknowledgment of your competence, efforts, and the like is most always appreciated, but a constant need for such acknowledgments can indicate a requirement for reassurance. This is especially true when you interpret a lack of compliments and praise as the other person pointing out your flaws and imperfections. You are using an absence (no positive feedback) to infer a negative (that they mean to indicate that you are flawed and imperfect) and, as a result, you may be very easily wounded by this irrational thought or belief. You may already be painfully aware of what you consider your flaws, hoping that others don't see them and needing compliments and praise to offset them. Failure to receive positive strokes leads to more wounding.

You may be primarily focused on external validation and acceptance rather than on self-validation and self-acceptance. Your attempts to hide, mask, deny, repress, and rationalize what you think are imperfections consume a lot of energy that could be better used to build your self, promote your self-acceptance, and change whatever behavior and attitudes really do need changing.

An Inability to Ignore Minor Irritation and Annoyance

One characteristic you may have that helps prevent you from letting go of negative or distressing feelings is an inability to ignore minor irritations and annoyances. Staying aware of when you have a negative feeling, such as irritation, can allow you to reflect on your feeling, judge the validity of the feeling as a threat to yourself, and realize that you don't have to keep the feeling if you don't want to. You could let go of the negative feeling, but if you don't it may continue to build and escalate.

Your inability to overlook, ignore, or let go of minor actions that produce feelings such as irritation and annoyance can be traced, in part, to what you think the triggering acts are saying about you. You become irritated or annoyed when you sense a threat to yourself. Most irritating and annoying acts present no real threat and can be overlooked or ignored. Further, holding on to these annoyances can have negative effects on your health, sense of well-being, and relationships. Try the following reflection to get started on thinking of ways you can ignore minor irritations and annoyances:

Sit in silence and think of a recent event that produced irritation or annoyance for you. Nothing major, just something small, but you still feel some discomfort when you think about it.

Recall what was done or said and write a sentence or brief paragraph that describes the irritating or annoying act. If you experienced something unspoken or not observable, like an attitude, try to capture that in a few words.

Now list what the act or attitude seemed to be saying about you. Don't focus on the other person, the validity of what was done or said, the right or wrong, and so on. Stay focused on what you thought or felt it said about you. You can also select from the following list if any fit:

- I'm stupid.

- I'm disgraceful.

- I'm not good enough.

- I'm not loved.

- I'm not valued.

- I'm not in control.

- I'm powerless.

- I'm helpless.

- I'm hopeless.

- I'm not appreciated.

- I'm not worthwhile.

- I'll be hurt, abandoned, or destroyed.

Give each thought and feeling a validity rating from 0 (no validity) to 10 (extreme validity), that is, how true is this thought or feeling. For example, if you wrote or chose "I'm stupid" as what the act or attitude seemed to be saying about you, you now rate the extent to which you think "I'm stupid" actually fits you.

Low validity ratings indicate that you perceived the act or attitude to say something negative about you, but that that is not how you actually perceive yourself. If you feel that there is little or no validity to the charge, you then need to ask yourself, "Why am I reacting to an untruth about me?" If the thought you were operating under at the time is really false, you can overlook or ignore it. It doesn't matter and it doesn't fit.

If you are still bothered even though you gave it a low validity rating, you may want to explore for yourself if you have a suspicion that there is some truth to what the act or attitude seems to be saying about you. You may also have that perception about yourself that the annoying event seemed to confirm. The same can be true if you gave it a moderate or high validity rating. This is something to work on, but you don't have to retain the irritation or annoyance.

Catching Others' Feelings

Do you find that you become distressed or upset when you are in the presence of someone who is sad, despairing, or otherwise upset? If you're around someone who is hostile or angry, do you become tense, say sarcastic things, or become curt and abrupt in your responses? Do you want to get away when interacting with people who are emotionally intense and find that you retain some anxiety even after leaving them? These are examples of how you can experience catching others' emotions.

You may be contributing to your distress by taking in others' pain, resentment, anger, fear, and the like. You tend to catch these feelings, they stay with you, you resonate with them, and you may become injured or reinjured. You are personalizing and identifying with someone else's feelings and find it difficult or impossible to separate your feelings from theirs or to let them go, so you remain mired.

Building your psychological boundaries will enable you to avoid catching others' feelings. You will still be able to be empathic with them, but you will not incorporate or identify with their feelings. You will also be able to let them have their feelings without falling prey to any of the following:

- Taking their feelings into your self and identifying with them, and thereby making their feelings your feelings and acting on them.

- Remaining mired in unpleasant feelings and unable to let go.

- Feeling that you are responsible for the other person's feelings.

- Trying to make the feelings go away for the other person so that that person will feel better, because this also allows you to feel better.

- Becoming upset yourself. While you may chide yourself on occasion, if you find that you are frequently upset with yourself, you may be acting on the feelings you catch from others, and you will want to work to eliminate that.

Developing strong and resilient boundaries is a process, and you may want to use the expertise and guidance of a competent therapist to work with you on this.

Feeling Flawed and Imperfect

Everyone has flaws and imperfections, but for a child of a self-absorbed parent these perceived flaws can be a considerable source of guilt, shame, and pain. Perceived flaws and imperfections may be realistic or irrational. An example of the latter is when someone feels compelled to be perfect in everything, and so when the inevitable happens and the person does something that is not perfect, that becomes an opportunity to engage in self-blame and have negative thoughts about oneself. This dynamic is in effect even when that person cognitively knows that perfection is an ideal and that most mistakes are not shameful. This is an example of the disconnect that can occur between logic and feelings.

Getting in touch with your flaws can set off some powerful emotions that go to the core of your inner essential self. After all, it is your essential self that defines you as a person, and you want to be proud of who you are. This is what everyone wants. Accepting that you have flaws and imperfections is a lifelong process that some people never really begin. They may say that they are self-accepting, but the reality is that they deny, repress, hide, and mask their true self because of what they perceive as unacceptable imperfections. You may not hide these from yourself, but you are painfully aware of them and this causes you some distress. You are constantly reminded that you have flaws and imperfections, but you also don't seem to be able to do what seems necessary to overcome them. This also causes you some distress.

If this characterization fits you, then you probably find it difficult to forgive others and impossible to forgive yourself for any lapses, mistakes, failures, and so on. You are as hard and demanding of others as you are of yourself and wonder why others don't work harder to overcome their flaws and imperfections. You don't understand how they can be so accepting of being less than perfect, because you can't do that.

A major part of building your self will be to become more self-accepting. That doesn't mean that you give up working to become a better person—it means that you have a different attitude and perception of yourself. You are able to focus on your strengths and positive attributes even though you remain aware of your flaws and imperfections. You'll learn some strategies to help with becoming more self-accepting in later chapters.

Needing Others to Be Like You

Although you may be aware of your flaws and imperfections, you may also be proud of some of your behaviors and attitudes. You may also wish that others had some of your characteristics because that would mean that you are not flawed—that you are validated and feel safer and more confident.

You may secretly think and feel that your way is the right way, and that the world would be a better place if people could only bring themselves to behave, think, and feel more like you do. All this may be true: you probably do have many behaviors and attitudes that deserve praise, you may be a role model in many ways, and you may rightly see how others could improve and be less troublesome. You have many positive characteristics and should be proud about these parts of yourself.

However, your thoughts about others being more like you can open you to injury when others don't seem to want those behaviors and attitudes, openly reject your attempts to get them to change, and don't find these characteristics as admirable as you do. It can feel like others are devaluing or rejecting you, not just choosing to think, feel, and behave in other ways. It is painful to feel that your self is rejected, and you don't see why they don't want to be more like you. Your reactions can range from shame about yourself for being devalued to rage and resentment about the person who is refusing to acknowledge that yours is a better and a more desirable way to be. Your reaction influences how you perceive and relate to that person.

What would be helpful for you is to recognize and accept that you cannot cause others to change, that there are other laudable attitudes and ways to behave, that others can find their own way to more constructive behaviors and attitudes, and that not being like you does not necessarily mean that others are wrong, bad, inept, or shameful. You will become less wounded when you can accept and appreciate others, even when they are different from you. This may be a major shift for you, but you can reduce and eliminate some of your wounding without giving up any of your admirable qualities.

Relationship Difficulties: Maintaining Meaningful and Satisfying Relationships

All relationships can go through some rough spots where you question your and others' commitment to the relation, or the relation's purpose, meaningfulness, or degree of satisfaction. You question these because of changes and life events. Another thing that can trigger you to question a relationship is a feeling of dissatisfaction. The dissatisfaction can be with yourself, the other person, conditions at work, or even life circumstances. You can begin to question your relationships for many and varied reasons. What is most important, however, is that your satisfaction and the relationship's meaningfulness be a part of your awareness.

Understanding Your Contributions to Continued Wounding

If you've read and engaged in the suggested reflections in this chapter, you now have some understanding of how you can or do contribute to your wounding. Yes, other people do say and do things that are mean, demeaning, and devaluing, but you don't have to let these things enter and hurt you. You don't have to hold on to the words and actions, letting them fester and affect you and your relationships in unconscious ways. You can just remember them, but not permit them to continue to upset and wound you. You can understand why you get hurt, build your inner self to better withstand these kinds of assaults, and let go of the negative feelings.

As I discussed before, the depth and extent of your narcissistic wounding are related to your early life events that produced the initial wounding. You may not have words to describe these events, you may not even remember them. That's not important for what this book is trying to do. Even if you could remember them, you cannot change them. The best you could do is to understand what happened and realize that these experiences don't have to continue to negatively affect you. The approach used here is to understand what kinds of events may have produced your initial wound, suggest how your current behavior and attitudes may contribute to your injury or reinjury, propose steps and techniques for personal development of your inner self, and provide a process for letting go. The work you've done so far in this book is the beginning of this process, and we will continue to develop skills and understanding to help you better manage these old scars and prevent further wounding.

Why Your Parent May Be Considered as Successful by Others

There are numerous reasons why self-absorbed parents can be considered as successful in other parts of their lives, such as at work or in the community, and you wonder why others cannot see and react to the parent as you do. Although there are many reasons for this, just three will be presented and discussed her: different experiencing, goal focusing, and indifference to others.

Different Experiencing: What Others Cannot See

Self-absorbed parents may present themselves differently to different people and in different situations or environments. In addition, other people have their own unique lens for perceiving and reacting to others. Depending on their roles and connections to your self-absorbed parent, other people may not see beyond the façade presented, and they may not realize that the parent acts and relates differently to you or others.

You may wonder at times why others do not perceive or react as you do to your parent, even when you try to describe that parent's behaviors and attitudes that negatively affect you. Or why others cannot see the parent's excessive and inflated self, aggrandizing behavior, entitlement attitude, and so on. Even if some others do notice such traits, they do not see them as frequently as you do, nor have they experienced the constant negative effects on their selves as you have. Others may be able to rationalize or excuse what they see, and others are able to ignore the problems or not even see them at all. What your self-absorbed parent does or says just does not impact or affect them, and they are able to walk away, while you cannot, even after all of these years.

Goal Focusing

Self-absorbed people are extremely goal focused for their personal needs and desires and wishes. Whereas being goal focused can help to better use one's time and energy most productively to accomplish a task or realize an accomplishment, many self-absorbed people use it to help them ignore others in the pursuit of their own goals. Sometimes, however, this goal focusing enables them to be successful, because they don't let anything or anyone get in the way of their efforts to achieve their goals.

Indifference to Others

You are probably aware of and pay attention to the impact of your behaviors and attitudes on others. But self-absorbed parents don't have this awareness as a personal expectation. That is, they don't care about what others think or feel, and their energies are focused on their own concerns and about getting what they want.

Self-absorbed parents may not be aware of or care about the impact of their behaviors and attitudes on others, but there are times when they think that it is in their best interests to act as if they are aware and care. For example, when self-absorbed people are trying to get something they want, and others can play a role in their achieving what is wanted, they may then become very attentive and responsive to others. They can be very good at reading others or guessing what others will respond to positively. They will use insincere compliments, over-the-top flattery, and misleading statements, they will convey gossip and lies about others, especially comments or remarks others make that can be twisted to suit their needs, and use other kinds of manipulative strategies because they feel entitled to get what they want by any means, and are unencumbered by caring about the impact they have on others.

CHAPTER ACTIVITIES

Writing: Focus on Your Strengths

Materials: A 3 by 5 index card, a writing instrument, and a suitable surface for writing.

Sit in silence and think about your personal strengths. Then construct a list of ten or more strengths that you have. Examples could include being organized, planful, humorous, a good cook, or anything else that you consider as a strength. Put the card away and review it each week.

Visualization: Hugs

Sit in silence in a place where you will not be disturbed or interrupted. Close your eyes (or, if that is distressing, keep them open). Try to bring up a picture of yourself when you suffered an incident that was hurtful. It does not have to be a major incident or hurt. Then, visualize you hugging and soothing yourself to reduce the hurt.

Drawing/Collage

Materials: a sheet of paper or cardstock, a set of crayons or markers or colored pencils; or a magazine from which to cut images, scissors, and glue.

Review the list of unproductive attitudes and behaviors in this chapter and select one that you want to change. Construct a drawing or collage that depicts the unproductive attitude or behavior and how you want to change it.

CHAPTER 4

Difficult Situations and How to Cope

Sylvia, her husband, and their children had stopped at her parents' home to wish them Happy New Year. Sylvia's mother met them at the door and her first words to Sylvia were to say how tacky Sylvia's clothes were and that her hair was a mess. Her mother then seemed to remember that the New Year had started and wished her son-in-law and grandchildren a Happy New Year. Sylvia was at a loss for how to respond to her mother, and felt angry and frustrated.

Why Situations Are Difficult

Difficult interactions with your self-absorbed parent can trigger your negative feelings such as anger, guilt, and shame. It would not be unusual for your responses to be ineffective because you are trying to protect your essential inner self while trying to think of an appropriate response. Difficult situations include ones where other people are present when your parent makes unfair comparisons or accusations, or belittles you, or makes comments designed to highlight your inadequacies. These situations can occur at family gatherings, or even at public events where you and your self-absorbed parent are present. Under these circumstances, some people, and maybe you, will try to get the parent to change their behavior, but this never works.

However, the failure seldom deters you from continuing this futile effort. This parent will not change because you want the parent to change, does not accept that they need to change, thinks that you're the one who needs to change, and is not reluctant to continually point this out to you, thereby exacerbating the effect on you. You will be much more effective and serene when you can accept that the parent will not change, when you build your essential inner self to be less unconsciously dependent on your parent, and when you are more centered, grounded, strong, and resilient.

Your feelings can be managed, whether they arise from within you or are projected by someone else and you incorporate and act on them. You can control what you feel, the feeling's intensity, and whether or not to verbalize or otherwise act on your feelings. You have more power over your feelings than you may think, and this power can help you navigate difficult situations and events with your self-absorbed parent. This chapter begins with some information about emotions so that you can begin to understand why you feel as you do and what you can do to control and manage your feelings, especially the negative ones that can be triggered by your self-absorbed parent. This understanding is basic to using the strategies you'll be learning later that can assist you in difficult situations.

Why You Feel as You Do

Feelings are a collection of sensations that your thoughts interpret and label, usually in relation to your inner essential self and its welfare. These sensations can be initiated by external and internal events, people, or situations, but it is your interpretations of these that determine what you feel. Most of this occurs on a nonconscious or unconscious level, and the factors contributing to your interpretations may not be fully understood.

Your analysis and interpretation of the sensations and the well-being of the self also lead to the decision about the resulting label for the feeling. For example, the interpretation of a threat to the self could lead to the feeling of irritation or annoyance rather than the related but more intense feeling of anger.

Being around your self-absorbed parent can trigger your old childhood feelings, such as helplessness, fear, or inadequacy. Although you are now an adult and react differently with other people, you may be unable to do so when you are in the presence of your parent, or even on the phone. In these instances, you may regress (go back) to feeling and reacting as you did in earlier interactions during your childhood. What can be more troubling for you and your relationships today is that you may be unconsciously reacting to what others say or do, or to what you *perceive* them to be saying or doing, as being similar to your parent. This is transference: a reaction to others that is not consistent with current reality but that is consistent with the past relationship with your parent.

The next section also presents a process and procedure for managing your negative feelings in interactions. A longer-term procedure will be presented in later chapters. When you feel unpleasant or scary emotions start to build as you read the book, take a moment to close your eyes and visualize a pleasant and calm scene, such as the one you created in chapter 2. This scene can also be used in interactions with your self-absorbed parent when you find that you are becoming upset. It may be helpful to practice retrieving the calming scene as much as possible, because this practice can make it easier and faster to access.

Containing and Managing Negative Feelings in the Moment

Following is a process to practice that can be effective in containing and managing your negative feelings as they occur in the moment. First, practice the process by thinking of an interaction with your self-absorbed parent and note what happens to the feelings you may still carry about that interaction. Next, try to memorize the steps. When you think that you are ready to implement the process, try it with someone other than your parent.

1. Accept the responsibility for the feeling you are experiencing, and do not think that someone else is causing you to feel as you do.

2. Identify and name the feeling, for example, anger, frustration, fear, guilt, or shame.

3. Identify the self-statement associated with the feeling. Self-statements are things like "I'm inadequate," "I'm incompetent," "I'm powerless," and "I'm shameful."

4. Assess the validity of the self-statement. For example, although you are not adequate all of the time, this does not mean that you are inadequate overall. So the self-statement about your adequacy is not valid.

5. Substitute a more positive and reasonable self-statement, such as "I am adequate much of the time." Notice how you feel when you make the positive self-statement.

6. If necessary, use your emotional insulation to block any negative projections that may be coming your way.

This is a process that can easily and quickly be used, especially if you practice the steps until you don't have to think about them. You will find that this process is very helpful in dealing with your self-absorbed parent and others who may be triggering negative feelings for you.

Difficult Situations and Suggestions

There are numerous difficult situations you may encounter with your self-absorbed parent, each unique to you and to your situation. It isn't feasible to try to present all such situations—they can be as varied as each person's experience. For ease of discussion they are grouped into categories: attacks, conflict, intrusive behavior, and special occasions.

Attacks on Your Essential Inner Self

Among the many ways that your self-absorbed parent can attack you are criticism, blame, and devaluing and demeaning comments. These attacks are injuring because they point out how the speaker perceives your essential inner self in very unflattering terms. Examples of such comments include the following:

"Why can't you ever (get it right, be more successful, look better, dress well, keep your hair fixed, and so on)?"

"You never (or you always)…"

"You ought to know (do, be, and so forth) better than that (this)."

"Your (sister, brother, cousin, acquaintance) can do (something). Why can't you be more like that person?"

The unexpected nature of the attacks on your essential inner self combined with the awareness of the presence of other people and the feelings triggered can affect your thinking and responding and make these less effective. What follows in the section below on conflicts can be used when you feel attacked. The suggestions are intended to give you choices of how to respond that will allow you to maintain civility and courtesy and to not get caught up in the negativity generated by your parent.

Conflicts

Conflicts can range from mild disagreements to battles. The most important point about conflicts is how they leave you feeling. Generally, conflicts with your self-absorbed parent arouse feelings that leave you upset, helpless, ineffective, and feeling wrong or inadequate. Think about it. Have you ever come out of such a conflict, even a mild one, feeling like a winner? Your answer is probably either no or seldom. You've also probably tried everything to avoid these conflicts, or to get your parent to see your perspective, or to make your parent aware of the impact on you, in the hope that knowing the negative impact would cause the parent to refrain from hurtful comments. Your efforts have not produced the desired results, but this failure may not prevent you from continuing to try to defend yourself.

Suggestion 1: Avoid conflicts. The first suggestion is to avoid conflicts with your self-absorbed parent. When you want to challenge your parent about something or respond to a challenge by the parent, first assess the importance of your "winning" if you were to engage the parent or accept the challenge. Even if winning is important for you, how important is it for you to "win" at this time?

If you decide to avoid the conflict or challenge, you can use one or more of the following: fogging, distraction, ignoring factual errors, and accepting a differing perspective.

Smile and fog the situation. "Fogging" means to obscure the discussion. Tactics for fogging include changing the topic, focusing on an irrelevancy, and bringing something offbeat into the conversation.

Become distracted, such as saying you need a bathroom break, checking with the babysitter, remembering something that needs to be taken care of or that you left in the car or at home (always try to leave something—important or unimportant). Any distraction will suffice.

Let parental errors of fact go, rather than trying to get the parent to agree with a correction. Your parent is unlikely to be able to admit any errors and your pointing them out or trying to correct these is unlikely to be received well and is more likely to arouse the parent's ire.

Let your parent have their own perspective. Mentally shrug your shoulders. But note that physically shrugging your shoulders in the parent's presence may be inflammatory. Don't try to get in a contest with the parent, because you cannot win, and engaging in a contest only makes things worse for you.

Suggestion 2: Leave others out of the conflict. The second suggestion is to *go it alone*, and don't bring others into the fray in an effort to gain support, agreement, or an ally. When you try to include others, it makes them uncomfortable and doesn't provide the support you were seeking. Seek support for your position later from someone like a friend or a therapist. Some time and distance may provide you with an opportunity to be more self-reflective, to reduce some emotional intensity, and to use your self-affirmations. If you feel that you need support for your position, such as reassurance that you are right and that your parent is wrong, explore this with a valued confidant or therapist who can maintain confidentiality.

Suggestion 3: Manage your feelings. The third suggestion is *to not show your feelings on your face at this time*—keep them private. Use your emotional insulation to prevent revealing your feelings at this time, because revealing them will not be helpful and can even be harmful to you. Your parent has never been moved by your feelings and may have turned them against you to make you appear even more wrong or inadequate, and you have usually been left feeling worse. Nothing has changed that would lead you to believe that your feelings will matter to your parent.

The other strategies you'll encounter in this book can also help prepare you to become more effective in handling conflicts with your parent. Your personality and unique needs will help you select the strategies that are most acceptable for you and that you can most effectively implement.

Unreasonable Demands and Intrusive Questions

Your self-absorbed parent may still expect you to be available when needed, even though you are an adult and have a life and other responsibilities. The parent may make unreasonable demands on you to do things that the parent could do, to be responsible for the parent's physical and emotional welfare, to always do what the parent wants you to do or to be what the parent wants you to be, to act on parental desires and wishes, and to accept the parent's authority without dissent. This self-absorbed parent seems to think that your responsibilities, such as a job or family time, should be secondary to whatever the parent thinks or wants. You may try to meet as many parental expectations and demands as you possibly can, but you can never give the parent enough, and trying to meet all of the parental demands may even be detrimental to other parts of your life.

Intrusive questions show a lack of understanding and respect for your boundaries, and put you in a position where you run the risk of offending if you do not immediately supply the desired answers. Intrusive questions are those that ask for intimate, personal, and sensitive information about yourself or others that you may not want to share. When faced with questions like these, you may need time to understand your own needs, desires, and wishes, and when engaged in an interaction, you cannot take the time you need to think about the best answer. You are too busy interacting and reacting. These types of questions can be used to put you on the defensive by seeming to illustrate how wrong or inadequate you are in some respect. The most irritating thing about intrusive questions is that there are unconscious internal pressures as well as external pressures to provide answers when questions are asked. It can be difficult to ignore or refuse to answer these, especially when they come from a parent.

Part of the problem with parental *unreasonable demands* and *intrusive questions* is the parent's inability or unwillingness to accept you as separate and distinct from the parent. When self-absorbed parents make these demands, they fail to understand that you are a functioning adult to be related to as an adult, and that those parents are exhibiting the self-absorbed attitudes of entitlement and exploitation. On your side, you may still be relating to your parent as if you were a child, feeling the need to comply with the parent's demands or questions and not knowing how to set reasonable limits for how the parent is to relate and behave with you. Mostly what you are dealing with are your feelings about disappointing your parent, not being a "good child," and being perceived as rude or disrespectful. These are difficult feelings to overcome. Some of the suggestions provided later in this chapter and in the remainder of the book may be helpful, but some challenges may need help from a competent therapist to build and fortify your essential inner self, so as to attain more complete separation and individuation.

Holidays and Other Celebrations

Do you have a fantasy about family holidays and other celebrations that involves your self-absorbed parent? Do you hope each time that your image will be fulfilled and that you will look back on the event with warm and fond memories, only to never have that fantasized holiday? Does your self-absorbed parent manage to do or say something every time to spoil the occasion for you?

Although you continue to hope that your fantasy will come true, it never has. But you still long for a good outcome and continue to attend holiday and other celebratory events with the self-absorbed parent. Using some or all of the suggestions presented in the book can begin to make these events more tolerable for you. However, what will be of most help is for you to give up the fantasy and yearning for meaningful changes in your parent.

The Aging and Dependent Self-Absorbed Parent

An aging, dependent parent is one of the most difficult situations you can encounter, because such a parent's self-absorption can become more acute because of real conditions, such as failing health or finances. Even under the best of circumstances, these conditions and concerns can be troubling for parents and their children. The self-absorbed parent can ratchet up the complaints, unreasonable demands, blame, and criticism. The lack of empathy and concern for the adult child's circumstances only adds to the distressful situation, and the parent's entitlement attitude can really exacerbate all problems.

Added to the parent's self-absorbed behavior and attitude can be your guilt, self-doubt, anger, and resentment, and your own lingering aspects of undeveloped narcissism. These, too, are difficult to experience and manage effectively. Your self comes under even greater assault as you try to deal with internal and external forces that surround the situation with the aging and dependent self-absorbed parent. There are several points to remember when you are faced with these circumstances:

- Your parent does have some real problems which could require your assistance.

- The parent becomes less able to cope with their tasks, and this is distressful for the parent.

- The parent can be extremely fearful about what the future holds, and especially fearful of having inadequate personal or financial resources to deal with it.

- The loss, or potential loss, of independence is very upsetting and frightening for the parent.

- The parent is not likely to change and become less self-absorbed.

- The roles of child and parent become reversed, unless the child had already been put in the position of being responsible for the parent's welfare.

Under these circumstances, it is extremely difficult to set limits on the extent of your responsibility and to feel that your actions are adequate. Most distressing are your resulting feelings, so you will have to recognize that you do have personal limits and realize what they are. You must avoid letting your lingering aspects of grandiosity color your thoughts and attitudes, convincing you that you must "fix" the problem, make it go away, or fully and completely satisfy your self-absorbed parent.

Protecting Your Children: Set Boundaries

This section is included because of the questions I have received from readers about this issue. They want to know how to protect their children from experiencing what they did, and they fear that the self-absorbed grandparent will now negatively affect their children. Just as your parent did not recognize your personal psychological boundaries, exploited and manipulated you, was not empathic, and so on, that parent may now exhibit the same behaviors and attitudes with the grandchildren.

The good news is that the grandparent will have less of an effect on the grandchildren, unless you are living in the same home with your parent. Distance, less contact, and your interventions can do much to minimize the negative effects on your children. Your empathy and understanding of what your children experience with your self-absorbed parent will be supportive and insulating for them. You can insulate your child from harm by making empathic responses to the child that demonstrate your understanding of the child's feelings. This is not taking your child's side against your parent—it is affirming and supporting your child. Other strategies include clear directions about treatment of the child, blocking inappropriate remarks to and about the child, not requiring unneeded apologies from the child, and affirming your child.

Communicate clear directions to your parent about how you want your child treated. For example, let your parent know that any transgression by the child should be brought to your attention for proper treatment, and that the grandparent should not punish or chide the child. Make sure the child also knows this.

Block demeaning, blaming, critical comments and remarks directed to and about your child, even if you have to take the heat yourself. You can block these by intervening and changing the topic, sending the child away to do or get something, interrupting your parent to praise your child for something, and other such behaviors. It will do no good to ask your parent to not make these remarks and comments.

Insist on the child *apologizing only when absolutely necessary,* not merely to keep the peace. Keep such apologies to a minimum. Teach the child how to present an apology in a way that is not shaming for the child but that also recognizes the offense and the impact on the parent. If the parent is offended but you do not understand that there was an offense or what the offense was, you can take the heat and present the apology yourself. Such apologies should focus on the unintentionality of the offense and state that you regret that there was an offense to the parent.

Affirm your child by praising them frequently in your parent's presence. While it is not necessary to give too many compliments, it is helpful to openly acknowledge when the child does something helpful or otherwise acts in a praiseworthy way.

If you need to ask the parent to look out for the child, keep such requests for babysitting or child management to a minimum, if you make them at all. You put yourself in your parent's debt when you ask for favors.

Be pleasant and cordial to your parent when intervening to keep the parent from acting in a way that would emotionally or psychologically injure your child, but do stand up for and support your child. Be concrete and firm with your intervention. No one should doubt that you are supporting your child.

If the parent starts to compare your child with anyone, immediately block any comparisons. You can comment something to the effect that all people have positive character-istics and talents, and that these are valued, and that it is not helpful to make comparisons.

Specific Strategies to Help

Presented below are some general strategies that can be used with all types of self-absorbed parents. First are three internal states to deal with. Second are four actions *not* to take. Last are eight constructive acts that can be helpful in difficult situations.

Three Internal States

It will be very helpful to try to reduce or eliminate these internal states that contribute to your emotional vulnerability: yearning and longing, wishing for change, and emotional susceptibility.

You may be able to reduce your yearning, longing, and wishing by becoming aware that these states are the roots for much of the discomfort you experience with your self-absorbed parent. You keep wanting your parent to be empathic, to like you and love you, despite all the evidence to the contrary. You have not been able to get empathy, liking, and love, but you keep wanting these and your unrealized desires make you vul-nerable to the parent's manipulation, exploitation, and control. You will help yourself a lot if you can relinquish these.

Much pain will disappear when you can accept that your parent is unlikely to become the parent of your dreams, is unlikely to change, and sees no need for changing. The reality is that your desire for the parent to change is futile. This doesn't mean that your parent doesn't love you. It does mean that the parent doesn't and can't love you in the way that you want or need. So it will serve you better if you can accept the fact that if the parent will not change, you can change.

Actions to Avoid

This next set of suggestions is focused on actions that you will want to work hard to avoid. These actions may be tempting to use because they can be a part of who you are or may provide some short-term satisfaction. Please do not use retaliation, empathizing with the parent, confrontation, or inappropriate disclosure. These actions do not help the situation, your relationship with your self-absorbed parent, or your feelings about yourself. They are counterproductive and are not constructive for your growth and development.

Retaliating. Retaliation occurs when you are hurt and do or say something designed to make the other person hurt as you were hurt. The short-term satisfaction does not last, the act can make the relationship worse, and in the end you haven't gained anything. The best retaliation or revenge is to build your self and to become successful in your own accomplishments and achievements. This is much more constructive and is also personally satisfying. This is known as positive revenge and is addressed in chapter 6.

Empathizing. Empathy is a deep resonance with another's experience without losing your sense of self as separate and distinct from the other person. Your parent probably does not empathize with you, and you may keenly feel this lack and long for your parent to be empathic. This may lead you to feel that you should, or must, empathize with your parent. You may even think that your empathy will help promote change in your parent. But when you try to empathize with your parent, you are more likely to open yourself up to incorporating your parent's negative projections and integrating these into your self, leaving you upset and unable to let go of the negative and uncomfortable feelings you've taken in. If you want to do something, you can sympathize, where you make comforting and reassuring comments that don't require you to also experience the feelings that go along with the words.

Confronting. I cannot emphasize enough the importance of not engaging in confrontation with your parent. Even if you are experienced in constructive confrontation, you would be ill-advised to try it with your self-absorbed parent. If you've made the attempt at a confrontation and you objectively and realistically recall the event, you are most likely to come to the realization that it didn't work. Not only was confrontation ineffective, but you were probably left with residual negative feelings that lingered. You left the confrontation feeling worse than before you started. Your parent is not open to your thoughts, feelings, and ideas; does not relate to or care about your feelings; does not feel a need to change anything about himself or herself; and may become enraged that you think that they are less than perfect. You cannot win, or even make any inroads into your parent's self-absorption.

Self-Disclosing. You may have disclosed personal and intimate thoughts and feelings to your parent or may have been tempted to do so. This too is not advised, because your parent is likely to use the information against you and your best interests. The results of disclosure can be that you are chastised or criticized, blamed for not being better, and the like. You may be demeaned for your thoughts and feelings, and your parent may compromise the confidence of what you have revealed, telling others what you've shared and thus leading to more discord or criticism. Keeping mum about sensitive issues and feelings doesn't require you to cut your parent off from your personal life altogether, but it does mean that some of the following would be helpful:

- Tell your parent only what you wouldn't mind being revealed to the world.

- Don't take your problems or concerns to your parent. Find a trusted confidant who is knowledgeable and can keep a confidence.

- When talking with your parent, minimize any concerns or problems you may have. Be as upbeat as possible.

Eight Helpful Actions

Here are eight suggested actions that can help you with managing and controlling situations and your feelings when interacting with your parent: build your inner self, block and control your feelings, restrict and manage interactions, use positive self-statements, capitalize on some nonverbal behaviors, choose what to feel, interrupt negative thoughts, and use self-talk as a reminder.

Building your inner self means that you develop empathy, creativity, inspiration, and relationships or connections. Doing so will enable you to let go of old grudges and resentments; have sufficient psychological boundary strength to lessen emotional susceptibility and judge what feelings are yours alone, uncontaminated with others' feelings; and better cope with your triggered feelings that are aroused in interactions with your self-absorbed parent.

Blocking and controlling your feelings is a strategy that can allow you to be calm when being blamed, criticized, demeaned, devalued, and the like, so that you can think and act more constructively. The feelings are still there, but they can become less intense, which then makes them easier to put aside for the moment. Blocking your emotions uses a personal strategy of momentarily removing yourself from the feeling, such as using thoughts, since thoughts are cognitive and thus easier to manage than are feelings. You can say to yourself that you will allow yourself to access these feeling later.

Manage interactions so as to ensure that most of your interactions with the parent that require more than a few minutes happen in public places, such as restaurants, entertainment venues, religious places of worship, and so on, rather than as a one-to-one interaction. It's usually easier for you to have your negative feelings triggered when interactions are prolonged, and when they take place among intimate family members (such as during holiday celebrations) or when you have to be alone with the parent. You can propose that events be held in public places; arrange any mandatory events, such as birthday parties, to include many nonfamily participants; and set reasonable time limits for your participation in these.

Positive self-statements will prevent you from getting caught up in intense negative emotions triggered by your self-absorbed parent. It can be important to remember that your triggered feelings are impacted when, on some level, you are buying into your parent's perceptions of you and you fear that these perceptions may have some validity. Self-affirmations remind you of your strengths and positive characteristics, so that you don't get mired in thoughts and feelings about your real or imagined flaws.

Capitalize on nonverbal signals, since you are less likely to catch your self-absorbed parent's negative feelings or to have your negative feelings aroused if you can do any or all of the following:

- Avoid eye contact, especially sustained eye contact, and angle your body away from the parent.

- If forced to look at the parent, focus on an ear, or chin, or the middle of the forehead.

- Put some physical object between you and your parent.

- Adopt a relaxed body position.

- Think about something pleasant or zone out.

- Keep a neutral or pleasant facial expression (but don't grin or frown).

These behaviors can effectively protect you from your parent's efforts to engage you. Try not to use nonverbal behaviors that are likely to arouse the parent's ire, such as those used by sullen adolescents (sulking, mumbling). You are not trying to get the parent angry, as that would increase the parent's focus on you and might just produce more negative comments. You are just trying to tolerate the situation for the moment.

Choosing what to feel may be a difficult concept to accept. It may appear to you that your feelings just emerge and that you have no control over them, but you do have the ability to decide what to feel, especially when you understand the roots of your feelings and have resolved some of your family-of-origin issues and past unfinished business. The next two sections describe some strategies that can help with this, but first you have to understand and accept that you can choose what to feel, and that you do not have to feel what your parent is trying to inspire in you, catch the parent's negative feelings, or unconsciously react as you did when you were a child.

Interrupt negative thoughts about yourself when they emerge. These can include self-criticism and blame, negative feelings such as shame and anger, and unrealistic ideas about yourself, such as the need for perfection. This strategy works best when you not only interrupt negative thoughts, but also substitute more positive thoughts, feelings, and ideas. When you are able to avoid having these negatives and can insert more positives, you become better able to tolerate interactions with your self-absorbed parent and will not be as vulnerable to getting mired in enduring and unpleasant thoughts and feelings about yourself.

If you are experiencing some negative thoughts about yourself at this point, stop reading and consciously interrupt them. This includes any "should" or "ought" statements, such as "I should not let my parent get to me." These are unproductive and unhelpful. Next, substitute a positive self-statement.

Use positive self-talk to remind yourself of what is real and what is fantasy. The line between these can become blurred, especially when intense emotions are involved. Your negative feelings are easier to control when you can introduce some realism and not get caught up in fantasy. Try answering the following questions to get some idea of how fantasy interferes with reality:

- Is it realistic to expect your parent to see that you were hurt and to expect your parent to try to make amends?

- Can your parent admit mistakes or accept their errors? If not, how realistic is it to point these out or to try to correct the parent's misperceptions?

- If you have not experienced empathy from your parent in the past, why do you expect it now?

All of these thoughts exhibit the yearning you have for a fantasized loving and empathic parent. Your longings are keeping the fantasy alive, contributing to your distress, and preventing you from mobilizing your resources to remain centered and grounded. These untapped inner resources could prevent you from being hurt any further.

Summary

In this chapter we looked at some common situations with self-absorbed parents that can be stressful and produce considerable discomfort. You learned strategies that can help reduce or eliminate some negative effects that these situations can produce.

CHAPTER ACTIVITIES

Writing

Materials: A 5 by 8 index card, a sheet of paper, and a pen or pencil for writing.

Procedure: Find a quiet place to work where you will not be disturbed and where you'll have a hard surface for writing, such as a table or large book.

1. Use the sheet of paper to list ten to twelve things you consider to be your accomplishments, such as holding a job, overcoming an illness or condition, rearing responsible children, and so on.

2. Next to each accomplishment, list all personality characteristics associated with the accomplishment. For example, for holding a job you might list persistence, determination, ambition, and organization.

3. Review the list of accomplishments and associations, and then construct another list that incorporates eight to ten personality characteristics that are repeated two or more times. These form the basis for your positive self-statements.

4. At the top of the index card, write "I am," and then write the list of repeated characteristics from step 3. These are your positive self-statements.

5. Read this card once a week until you can effortlessly recall the items *when you are experiencing intense negative emotions*, such as those experienced in interactions with your self-absorbed parent.

Drawing/Collage

Construct a collage of a treasured major accomplishment of yours.

Visualization

Visualize yourself accepting an award for an accomplishment. Who is present? How big is the award? Are there cameras? What is the action?

CHAPTER 5

Identify and Overcome Hidden Toxic Effects of Your Parent

Brian was an engineer at a major corporation that had branches all over the world. He worked hard and put in long hours to make sure he did everything well, to the point where almost all he was doing was working and taking a few hours to sleep and eat. He did not have a family or social life, and he even worked on holidays. Although he was entitled to vacations, he never took them. If he asked himself why he worked so hard, his response would have been something like, "To make sure I'm good enough."

Hidden and Disguised Toxic Effects

Even though you may have forgotten some parental injuries to your essential inner self, repressed or denied some, or refused to think about them, they can exert hidden and disguised effects that are toxic. They affected your self-confidence, your self-efficacy, and your self-perception, all of which can have negative effects on you and your relationships. A significant part of building your self will be to detoxify.

Previous chapters have discussed how wounding occurs and how the initial wound can continue to fester, how you can be rewounded, and how this produces toxic buildup. At this point you may be more aware of how some of your family-of-origin experiences and other past experiences produced the initial wounding. You may also be aware of how your personal characteristic beliefs about your essential inner self prevent you from defending that inner self against becoming rewounded, and contribute to your inability to heal and grow. This awareness and understanding is helpful and may even help you see where you can make constructive changes.

Possible Toxic Effects on You

We now turn to discussing other possible effects on you that you did not know were outcomes from the injuries on your essential inner self. Read the following statements and rate the extent to which each describes you using this scale: 5: very much descriptive of me. 4: descriptive of me. 3: sometimes descriptive of me. 2: very little descriptive of me. 1: not descriptive of me at all.

1. I have high to extremely high levels of stress much of the time.

2. I am or have been told that I am easily irritated and frequently cranky.

3. I frequently experience disturbed sleep, such as disquieting dreams, or insomnia.

4. Much of the time I feel out of sorts or off balance.

5. I am often distracted, have a lack of focus, and find it difficult to concentrate.

6. My overall enjoyment is usually deflated.

7. I have a lot of intrusive unpleasant thoughts.

8. I am usually disorganized.

9. I have considerable dissatisfaction with my physical self.

10. My relationships are not satisfying or enriching.

11. Life's meaning and purpose is often missing or not satisfying.

12. I am very dissatisfied with my accomplishments.

Add your ratings to get a total score. Scores 51-60 may indicate a very high level of toxicity; 41-50 may indicate a high level; 31-40 may indicate a moderate level; 21-30 may indicate that there is some toxicity; and scores of 20 or below indicate little or no toxicity.

Toxic buildup increases the possibility that your wounded self is unable to heal or to protect itself. Toxic buildup can affect all aspects of your being and of your life. The rest of this chapter will focus on understanding how your behavior and attitudes can be reflective of some toxicity and provide suggestions for detoxification.

There are many ways to handle toxicity, such as over- or undereating, substance abuse, staying in an abusive relationship, depressed episodes, and suicidal thoughts. Using such ineffective or even destructive ways will only add to your distress, or at best provides surface momentary relief. Then, too, you may not be aware that your self-destructive behaviors are an unconscious attempt to handle your toxicity. Some of these behaviors and attitudes can actually be destructive to your self-esteem and to your relationships. As you read the descriptions for these, try to assess how much you may be using the particular behavior or attitude, and stay open to the possibility that you may be doing this without conscious awareness. Other unconstructive conscious and unconscious behaviors and attitudes for handling toxic buildup include defense mechanisms, acts against one's self, and acts against others.

Defense Mechanisms

These are unconscious mechanisms for protecting the self. The five that are presented in this section—displacement, repression, denial, withdrawal, and projection—are not all the defenses that can be used, but they may serve as good examples. Although defense mechanisms are unconscious, you can recognize them in retrospect, become more aware of your tendency to use them, and start to analyze what you are protecting your essential inner self against. In other words, you can learn to better evaluate threats and dangers to your essential inner self, and thereby reduce your tendencies to employ your defenses. You may find that you are employing defensive mechanisms from a nonexistent threat.

Displacement is often used when you cannot directly attack a particular target. Rather than taking whatever it is on yourself, you put it on another target that is safer to attack. Family members are often the latter targets. You've probably heard the example of a workman getting yelled at by his boss, becoming angry, going home, and yelling at his wife for some minor or nonexistent act. That's displacement. It was not safe to attack the boss, so the anger got displaced onto the spouse.

Reflection: Think about an incident when you were unfairly accused, treated disrespectfully, or ignored, or when you felt minimized or dismissed and were not in a position where you felt you could protest or complain about the treatment. Now, reflect on what you did with your feelings about your treatment. Is it possible that you later displaced the feelings and reactions you had at that time onto someone else?

Repression is a defense mechanism that will be difficult for you to recognize in yourself. You will have to suspend disbelief for a while and accept that you most likely have engaged in repression. Accepting this should not be difficult. Everyone has forgotten something only to remember it at a later time. That is an example of repression.

What happens during repression is that a distressing incident is buried so deeply that conscious thought cannot access it, or at least cannot access many of the details. What happened was so personally threatening that you want to make sure that you don't have to be aware of it. No amount of thinking or reflecting or of someone telling you about it can make you recall it. However, just because it is buried doesn't mean that it doesn't continue to affect you in numerous ways, because its influence is also on an unconscious level. For example, a dislike for someone that you cannot explain could be because of some repressed material about that person, about a similar situation, or even about someone else from your past.

Reflection: Have you ever heard a story from a parent, sibling, or relative about a past event where you were present but you did not recall anything about the event? Did this event also have some distressing and negative aspects? You may have repressed memories about the event because it was personally distressing and maybe even traumatic for you. Trauma is very commonly repressed.

Denial is an unconscious mechanism that protects you from unacceptable and unpleasant truths about yourself. It is not a simple disagreement with what someone else is saying about you. What they say may be accurate or inaccurate, but in either case you don't have to agree with it. The form of denial we are talking about here is deep-seated, inaccessible to you, and you don't know if it is valid or invalid. Your self has decided that it is much too dangerous for its continued survival for you to be aware of or accept whatever is hidden.

Denial as a defense is used for everything and by everyone. What happens is that people cannot see or accept that their behavior is self-destructive, or out of control, and that it is destructive to them or their relationships. To admit the destructiveness of the behavior is much too threatening to the essential inner self. They will argue that they can stop or control the behavior at any time they choose to, but this is not actually true and they refuse to admit it. No amount of telling, selling, insisting, or browbeating can get through to them because it is too threatening to the self to admit this weakness, lack of control, and shame.

Reflection: Are there aspects of your life where you are in denial? For example, an abusive relationship, eating too much or too little, refusal to take needed medicine or to seek medical help, aversion to seeing a mental health professional for your depression, overspending to gain attention and admiration, and illegal acts are some things other than addictions that can cause denial.

Withdrawal can be both conscious and unconscious, but in either case it is a defense mechanism, and is usually an emotional or psychological flight from the present danger. While physical withdrawal is usually a conscious act, psychological and emotional withdrawal is more likely to be on a nonconscious or unconscious level.

Unconscious withdrawal causes you to be inaccessible to other people. You simply are not there in spirit, although you may there in body and interacting. Your self is elsewhere for its own survival and safety. Others, especially those who know you well, may sense this withdrawal, but you can remain unaware of what you are doing. Some indications of withdrawal are: mind wandering, day dreaming, mentally planning for a future act, and returning to a past event.

What can be helpful for you when you recognize or become aware that you are withdrawing is to try to recall what was happening when you phased out. There was something going on in your environment that signaled that your self was threatened in some way, and so you took flight. That something was shaming, guilt producing, overwhelming, revealing of your inadequacies, and so on. You felt powerless to control and manage whatever was triggered for you and you just decided to leave.

Reflection: When you are in unpleasant situations and have a strong desire to be somewhere else, so as to not engage in conflict, or feel intense and negative feelings, do you let your mind go elsewhere so that you do not have to engage or experience the negative and intense feelings?

Projection was defined in an earlier chapter as getting rid of something unacceptable about your essential inner self by unconsciously projecting it on to another person, and then reacting to that other person as if that person had exhibited what was projected. For example, if you were angry, you might project that anger onto another person as if that person was the one who was angry. This is another way in which your self can be protected from an unpleasant awareness.

Your shame, guilt, inadequacies, fears, and other negative, upsetting, and dangerous aspects of your self can be managed by putting them onto another person. You then have verification for how you respond to that person, since that person now seems to you to have the unacceptable characteristic that you cannot admit to yourself that you have. You don't accept it in your essential inner self, and you cannot accept it in the other person.

Such projections can negatively affect your perceptions of others, promote mistrust, and erode relationships of all kinds. Your view of reality is distorted, and even if that distortion is slight, you remain unaware of what you are doing. The other person is usually unaware that they are the recipient of your projections, and does not understand your reactions. Some people are aware that they may be projecting, but most people will never ever consider that possibility.

You are overlooking, or not accepting, the awareness and acceptance about your essential inner self for the moment and for this situation. That past still remains with you and it is hidden. Because it is unconscious, you are unaware of the hidden effects on you and on your relationships.

Reflection: Think about a situation where you had a strong negative reaction to what someone said, did, or seemed to be. Ask yourself if your reaction was entirely or partly based on your projection. That is, if you reacted to what seemed to be anger in the other person, could that have happened because you projected your anger onto that person so that you would not have to experience it or to admit that you yourself were angry?

Acts Against Oneself

Acts against oneself include self-blame, despair, hopelessness, helplessness, and devaluing oneself. These are termed as acts against self because they tend to be hurtful or destructive things that you do to yourself. Others do not do them or cause them, you yourself instigate and carry them out. You have control over them, although you may not realize it. You may have operated so long under the dictates and perceptions of your self-absorbed parent that you don't realize that you do not have to think, feel, or react in these self-injuring ways.

Self-blame is not always destructive, even though it hurts. You may blame yourself for failures to live up to your expectations for yourself. But self-blame can be destructive when your expectations are unrealistic, such as expecting personal perfection; or when you don't have a good understanding of the limits of personal responsibility, such as when you think you are supposed to make sure that other people don't suffer any discomfort; or when you have failed to examine your values and unconsciously and unquestionably accepted those values espoused by your parents or your culture.

Reflection: How often do I blame myself for things over which I have no control? Can I remember to stop the blame and vow to do better next time? Can I applaud my successes or even recognize them? You bet you can!

Despair is very much like depression, but it may not have the physical cause that depression often does. Despair is a deflated spirit where your inability to have things go your way is very upsetting to you. It can result when you are unable to manage and control your essential inner self, your environment, or your relationships over a period of time and you fear that things will never get better for you.

Your sense of self-efficacy is determined in large part by your ability to get your needs met. Now, this does not say anything about the reasonableness, logic, and rationality of your needs. It only speaks to your getting them met. In fact, your needs can be reasonable or unreasonable, logical or illogical, rational or irrational, and can still be met or not met. What seems to be important is that you think you have enough ability and influence to get them met. That's what self-efficacy means. Despair can result when you believe that you cannot act or have someone act to meet your needs. If this description fits you, the suggestions in chapters 9 and 10 may be helpful.

Reflection: How do you give in to despair? Or how do you resist giving in to despair even when it seems that everything is working against you?

Hopelessness. Closely aligned with despair is hopelessness, which is defined here as an inability to imagine that things can ever get better. It is not so much a deflation of the spirit as it is a lack of visualization, imagination, realistic wishing, and knowledge. You cannot see your way out, or how to "fix it," or how you can be rescued. There is no hope.

This lack of hope can contribute to depression and despair. There are studies on the mind-body connection that point to the negative physical effects of hopelessness. You can really contribute to your own physical, emotional, spiritual, and relational lack of well-being when you lack hope.

There are situations where it is almost impossible to foster and maintain hope, such as a terminal illness, death of a loved one, conviction of a crime, or diagnosis of a chronic condition. No amount of hope will change these circumstances, and it is unrealistic to hold out false hope. However, one does not have to become hopeless, because there are other aspects of oneself and one's life that have potential for hope. You may not be able to change your circumstances, but you do have some influence and control over how you react to them. You also have a responsibility to take care of yourself as best you can, and being hopeless is not helpful to your self-care.

Reflection: What have I given up on as I've become hopeless? What may I be missing because of my hopelessness? What can I do to be more hopeful in other parts of my life?

Helplessness is discussed separately from hopelessness because it has more negative connotations for self-perception than does hopelessness. Lack of hope carries with it an implication that there are some outside influences that are preventing the person from being effective, whereas helplessness is totally within the person. This person, at this time, does not have the wherewithal to be effective. Thus, helplessness is seen as a personal inadequacy, and as failure.

Examples of helplessness include feeling, saying, or doing the following:

- Not knowing what to do or say that would be helpful to another person.

- Seeing an injustice or unfair act, but not being able to stop it.

- Being unable to prevent abusive acts on your self.

- Disappointing yourself or someone else.

- Repeating the same mistake, such as choosing intimate partners who betray you.

All these examples are focused on you and your inability to be effective, for if you were different, better, good enough, les flawed, and so on, you would not have to experience feeling or being helpless. At least that is what you probably tell yourself. What you are overlooking or ignoring is that feeling helpless is a signal or indication of where you need more personal development, better skills, a deeper understanding, or a more realistic appraisal of your abilities and expectations for your essential inner self.

Responses to feeling helpless fall into one of five categories: giving up, leaving, persisting, blaming outside factors, and building the self. Giving up and letting events take their course may be a response that mires you deeper in your sense of helplessness, or it may be a realistic appraisal of the situation. Leaving is a form of withdrawing to protect yourself from having to confront your helplessness. When you persist and keep trying to be effective, it could bear positive results, or you could just be trying over and over again what did not work the first time. It is really amazing how often all of us do something that does not work, did not work, and will not work, but we persist. Blaming outside factors for your helplessness is a common response, and is seen in the defense of rationalization. It is also possible that outside factors actually are a barrier or constraint. The most positive response is to build your essential inner self, so that when you feel helpless, you know that you actually are helpless, as opposed to overlooking some personal resources that would be effective in these circumstances.

Reflection: What is my response to feeling helpless? How can I recognize my underused personal resources to be more effective? Am I being realistic about myself and the situation when I experience helplessness? Am I looking for someone to rescue me?

Devaluing yourself is a particularly destructive response to toxic buildup. The world confronts you every day with your inadequacies, ineffectiveness, lack of ability, and other negative qualities. When, in addition to these, you yourself fail to appreciate your positive qualities, this failure only increases the negative effects on your essential inner self.

The roots of your devaluation of yourself are located in your early family-of-origin experiences together with your other past experiences. Your self-perception is most heavily influenced in its development by the reactions to you by others in your environment, that is, your family and other significant people in your world. Early on you internalized some negative self-perceptions and these led you to devalue yourself. You may even focus more on what you perceive to be negative personal qualities than on your positive ones.

Devaluing is not a form of modesty, being self-effacing, or shunning the limelight. It is much more negative than these, and if you give any of these as an excuse, you are fooling yourself. You can be any or all of these without devaluing yourself.

Reflection: Become aware of devaluing yourself, either to others or to yourself. How often do you minimize your qualities, actions, and achievements? Are you fearful of being thought of as arrogant or boastful? How can you strike a balance between these two sides and become more appreciative of your strengths and other positive qualities without appearing arrogant or boastful?

Overvaluing yourself can also result from toxic buildup, when you protect your essential inner self from shame and feeling inadequate by inflating your characteristics, actions, and accomplishments. In this instance bragging and playing one-upmanship are common behaviors and attitudes. Cutthroat competition, jealousy, envy, power struggles, and other negative reactions are examples of overvaluing oneself, and doing so hurts you, others, and your relationships. All these can result from perceiving a strong need to protect your essential inner self.

These are some of the behaviors and attitudes that can be a reflection of overvaluing oneself:

- Never admitting mistakes or errors, as if you never commit these.

- Feeling that you would not make errors if others did what they were supposed to do, so any errors are their fault.

- Thinking that your contributions are of more importance than others are, and inflating your contributions or discounting those of others.

- Failing to accept personal responsibility.

- Continually boasting and bragging about your accomplishments, possessions, and so on.

These behaviors and attitudes are associated with underdeveloped narcissism and the fears of abandonment and destruction. The inability to understand and accept that others are also worthwhile and unique, together with the need to protect the self from imagined dangers, leads to self-absorption that negatively affects your relationships and prevents growth and development for those parts of your essential inner self that need them.

Reflection: Are any, or most, of these behaviors and attitudes reflective of me? Have I been criticized for any of these? Could it be that I cannot see these behaviors and attitudes as reflective of me? Am I refusing to see or admit that some of these are descriptive of me?

Acts Against Others

The third category for possible hidden toxic effects is acts against others, the things you do or say that are unconsciously intended to offload your shame, guilt, inadequacies, and fears. Needless to say, these behaviors are destructive to relationships, do not succeed in getting rid of your unwanted feelings and perceptions about yourself, and do not assist in constructive personal development. Acts against others include blaming, acting out, taking advantage, unreasonable demands, and devaluing and demeaning remarks, such as sarcasm and put-downs.

Blaming others for their mistakes and inadequacies in order to keep you from admitting your responsibility is a common response to toxic buildup. It is much easier to see others' faults, flaws, and errors than it is to see your own. It is also easier to point these out, in the hope that you will not have to be a part of whatever went awry. Further, blaming others is a way to show your superiority and their inferiority.

Yes, others do make mistakes, are inadequate, and so on. No one is disputing that. However, your tendency to blame others goes beyond noticing these faults, flaws, and errors. You are trying to shame the blamed person and to make that person feel guilty. Just think of how you feel when you are blamed whether justly or not. You feel shame for not being good enough, guilt for not living up to your standards, anger that the other person pointed this out, and fear that, because you were found wanting, you will be abandoned or destroyed. Now, you may say that you don't feel this intensely, but you are most likely to feel it at some level. The person you blame will have similar feelings and reactions. Even if that person is to blame, your pointing it out does not help the relationship or the situation.

Your tendency to blame others may be a result of your family-of-origin and other past experiences, when you observed others who were blaming and are imitating that behavior.

Some people who are blaming are projecting their personal feelings of shame and the like. So it becomes more difficult for you to know why you are blaming. It can be helpful for you to realize that blaming is neither constructive nor helpful for many circumstances.

Reflection: How often do I, verbally, or nonverbally, try to blame others? Can I become more aware of when I want to blame and refrain?

Acting out is a term used in therapy to cover a variety of defiant, oppositional, disruptive, and other distressing behaviors. An example of acting out is when you interrupt an existing conversation and change the topic so that you take over, become the focus of attention, and trigger some feelings in the people you interrupted. The following story is another example.

> An experienced high school teacher was taking a class at a local university to update her teaching certificate. As she reported later to her sister, she behaved uncharacteristically and badly in the class by chewing bubble gum and blowing a bubble, and by giving the instructor another student's name as her own. She seldom chewed gum of any kind, and did not allow chewing gum in her high school classes. She told her sister that she could not imagine why she behaved as she did. Her sister asked her how she felt about the class, and she responded that she was resentful about having to give up her free time to take the class. The subject and the teacher were okay, but she really did not care for the requirement that she take the class. This was a vivid acting out of the resentment, about lack of control over use of her time.

There are numerous ways to act out that irritate and annoy but that may not be serious enough for anyone to bring them to your attention, such as breaking or ignoring minor rules, deliberately failing to follow directions or guidelines, sulking, using indirect attacks, failing to cooperate, and thinking of how to retaliate. Instead of respectful and cooperative actions, acting-out behavior signals the opposite.

Reflection: Could some of my behaviors be "acting out"? I need to become more aware of the possibility that I am being resistant, defiant, and oppositional at times and work to understand what triggers this response for me.

Taking advantage refers to exploitation of another person or persons for your gain. You, perhaps unconsciously, have a need to show your superiority, power, control, or manipulative ability, and you do this at the expense of other persons. Taking advantage demonstrates your contempt for those other person, implying that they are weak, unworthy, and of lesser value.

You may think that you never take advantage of someone in this way, and perhaps you are right. But if you do any of the following, you are taking advantage:

- Telling a child to do something for you that you could do for yourself, such as getting the child to fetch something.

- Making plans or social engagements without consulting with your spouse, partner, or other family members.

- Putting your name on reports and the like when you contributed little or nothing to their development.

- Taking what others have, or what they give you, with no reciprocation.

- Expecting to receive preferential treatment all or most all of the time.

Such exploitive behavior is a characteristic of underdeveloped narcissism, where the person has not yet developed an acceptance and tolerance for other people as worthwhile and unique persons. Instead, such people think of others as extensions of themselves and thus consider others as under their control. It can also be a result of toxic buildup, where you are revenging the hurts you received by making others suffer, and this is used to shore up your self-perception.

Reflection: If I take advantage of others, this is not what I want to continue, is it? How can I become more aware of when I do this and what do I need to do to stop doing this?

Unreasonable demands. You probably think that any or all demands you make are reasonable ones. Otherwise you would not make them. But you need to suspend judgment for a little while and take a good look at what you demand from others, how you communicate these demands, how you react when they are met or not met, and the impact of these on others and on your relationships.

What demands are unreasonable? Although you may think that you are simply making requests, verbalizing your wants and needs, pointing out needed behavioral changes and attitude changes others should make, and trying to make things better, you are more likely to be demanding that these be done in accordance with what you think. Demands are unreasonable when they require any or all of the following:

- You expect other people to change because you want them to change.

- You expect other people to read your mind and to give you what you want, desire, or need.

- You expect others to stop doing something just because you don't like it or it makes you uncomfortable, and you expect them be alert to any sign that you are upset or distressed.

- You expect attention or admiration from everyone or almost everyone.

- You expect preferential treatment for yourself most all of the time.

- You expect others, such as your children, to order their lives as you want them to.

- You expect others to maintain their dependency on you.

These unreasonable demands are intended to order and control your world, and this need of yours could be a hidden or masked response to your toxic buildup. When other people do not meet your demands, ignore them, or term them as unreasonable, you encounter more toxic buildup. In this way, you continually reinforce some unconscious self-perceptions about your efficacy and worth.

Reflection: How can I become more independent? Can I try to think of others as independent to do or not do what they want, just as I wish this for myself? What can I do to reduce or eliminate what may be my unreasonable demands?

Devaluing remarks and actions. Just as with some other behaviors and attitudes previously described, devaluing and demeaning remarks and attitudes are intended to demonstrate your superiority, power, and control. These remarks and actions are used to show the other person as inferior, flawed, shamed, of lesser value, inept, and so on, and that you are none of these. Sometimes these remarks may be offered under the guise of being helpful to that person, as if that person didn't know any better and you are rescuing them, and your demeaning remarks may be disguised with an element of humor. Other rationalizations are often used so that you can fool yourself into thinking that you are not harming the other person.

Motives for such remarks or actions include projection and revenge. You may be projecting something unacceptable in yourself onto the other person so that you can openly reject that something. In that way you do not have to deal with your awareness of that unacceptable part of your essential inner self, and can let everyone around know that you don't like whatever it is by your devaluing or demeaning remarks about the person on whom you projected it. Revenge can also be an unconscious motive, where you are attacking someone else because of hurts you received earlier in your life.

There are no positive reasons or outcomes for devaluing and demeaning remarks and actions. They do not foster development of a positive relationship, and they don't endear you to the target of your remarks or to anyone else who observes them. People around you are more likely to have sympathy for your target and to think less of you. Try to become aware of when you may use any of the following and make a conscious effort to stop:

- Sarcastic remarks and comments.

- Put-downs.

- Jokes at others' expense.

- Deliberately misleading or misinforming someone.

- Making critical comments about others, either to their face or behind their back.

- Criticizing others about their clothes, body, hair, or possessions.

- Suggesting that someone is incompetent, inept, and the like.

- Reminding people of their past mistakes.

- Failing to show respect to another person.

Reflection: Do I sometimes consciously or unconsciously demean or devalue some people? How do I deal with my need to feel superior, powerful, and in control when I am with others? Is my essential inner self so needy or weak that I must devalue others in order to feel adequate or superior?

Summary

In this chapter, you most likely discovered one or more ways that you could be exhibiting results of hidden toxic buildup, and found some suggestions for needed changes. The next two chapters focus on strategies for detoxifying your essential inner self, building your essential inner self with strong and resilient boundaries, and how you can let go of the negative experiences and feelings that formed the toxic material. We have begun the process by helping you to become more aware of the toxic effects, both the obvious ones and the not so obvious ones.

To change any or all of these responses to toxic buildup requires thought, self-awareness, time, and effort. They took some time to insinuate their effects into your life, and it will take time to change them. Be patient with yourself, forgive lapses and errors, resolve to do better next time, and stay in touch with and be pleased about your positive accomplishments.

CHAPTER ACTIVITIES

Writing

Materials: A sheet of paper, a writing instrument, and a suitable surface for writing.

Find a place to work that is free from disruptions and interruptions. Make a list of five to seven "soul warmers": sights, sounds, activities, and so on that touch you deeply and that can be inspiring. Examples could include receiving an unexpected but affirming hug, hearing about an exciting accomplishment for a beloved family member who is on the right path, or feeling connected to the universe.

Draw/Collage

Select one of your soul warmers to illustrate with a drawing or collage. The drawing or collage could be symbols or images associated with the soul warmer, not necessarily a realistic depiction.

Visualization

Allow the vision of a happy moment to emerge. That moment could be real, imagined, or one that is wished for.

CHAPTER 6

Eight Strategies to Stop Hurting and How to Get Positive Revenge

Sara did not usually engage in self-reflection to examine her thoughts and attitudes about herself. So when she did have negative thoughts about herself, she just usually became depressed, feeling that she was fatally flawed and that others could see all of her flaws. But one day while she was once more thinking about how her father criticized her about practically everything when she was growing up and how he continued to do so even today, she realized that she did not automatically start thinking about how inadequate she felt in comparison to others. She also realized that she wasn't buying into some of her father's criticisms, she had thought of those possible flaws and noted them, but she was no longer obsessing over them. It seemed to Sara that she did not hurt as much when she thought about her father's criticisms of her.

Introduction

The most constructive and enduring strategy for lessening or eliminating the negative effects of the self-absorbed parent on you is to develop a stronger and more resilient essential inner self that not only allows you to have better interactions with that parent, but also enhances your other relationships. Constructive strategies are more rewarding in the long run than continuing to try to get your parent to change, which is seldom if ever successful. Turn your time, effort, and emotional investment to developing your essential inner self.

The remainder of this book is focused on presenting information and strategies you can use to build an essential inner self that is hardy, strong, resilient, and capable of initiating and maintaining meaningful and satisfying relationships—an inner self that does not continue to suffer the ill effects of a self-absorbed parent.

Eight Strategies That Can Help

First, let's begin with a celebration of the progress you've made, even if you are not where you want to be at this time. As you've worked through these chapters, you've probably shed some resentments and grudges and gained more awareness and understanding. Take a moment to celebrate this progress. Look at how far you've come, not how far you have to go. Take inventory of how your body and emotions seem, now that you are not carrying that baggage. Also, celebrate events where the emotional intensity has lessened. That, too, is progress and should be applauded. Knowing that progress is being made, albeit slowly, can be a motivator.

Here, now, are the eight strategies:

- Give up the fantasy that you will get the loving parent you long for.

- Develop positive self-talk and affirmations to use when you feel down or distressed.

- The role of altruistic acts in building the ideal self.

- Understand how reaching out to others can be encouraging and supporting.

- How to use a change of pace at times to revitalize yourself.

- The rewards for finding beauty and wonder in your everyday life.

- The positive effects of mindfulness in your life.

- The rationale for trying to eliminate your personal self-absorbed behaviors and attitudes.

These strategies are related to building your essential inner self, so that you are less likely to be wounded by things your parent says and does. They will help to heal old hurts, so that you can view them more objectively from your stronger and better protected self, and permit you to let go of negative feelings associated with old wounds. You can detoxify your essential inner self so that you reduce or eliminate defenses and stop committing acts against your self and acts against others.

You may feel that you have gained some understanding of yourself and of your parent after reading the first five chapters of this book. You may also still feel wounded from past actions by your self-absorbed parent and have identified how you took in some of that parent's negativity that caused you to think that you are not good enough and how you may be continuing to let this negativity affect your thoughts and feelings about yourself. While it may be tempting to continue to focus on the wounding that occurred, you will find it much more rewarding to focus on this wounding and toxic buildup, and to put your focus and energy on more constructive endeavors. The remaining chapters can guide you to learn what you can do to feel better today, to promote your inner development, to fortify your essential inner self, and to manage interactions with your parent.

Strategy 1: Letting Go of Fantasy

Let's turn to some constructive things you can do to handle your toxic buildup. The first strategy is to let go of fantasizing. This may be difficult to do since you may not even be aware that you are fantasizing, that you have a fantasy about your wounding events and your self-absorbed parent. Many fantasies have one or more of the following scenarios:

- Your parent admits their errors, hurts, and the like, and makes amends.

- Your parent suffers because of what they did to you.

- You are able to outperform your parent and can rub your parent's nose in your superiority and success.

- Everyone around your parent sees your parent as you do and rejects that parent.

- You are vindicated.

- You are able to do to the parent what was done to you, or someone else does that to the parent and you know about it.

- Your parent will change and have regrets about their words and actions.

These fantasies are helping you to retain your negative feelings, and these negative feelings reinforce the fantasies. They are fantasies because they are unlikely to happen just because of your wishing. Neither your parent nor anyone else is going to change because you want them to change. The other person may perceive events and situations differently than you do and be unaware or insensitive to your wounding. Your wishes, dreams, and fantasies about your self-absorbed parent are not helpful at all.

These fantasies result as reactions to your wounding and can have varying levels and intensities depending on the depth of the wound to your essential inner self. The stronger reactions are usually found for the deepest hurts. You may want to examine the events and your reactions for more understanding and awareness of what caused your most intense reactions. It is possible that you did not realize how much you were wounded by what was done or said until you gave this a high rating. That is, you thought that it was a minor event or that you were mildly or moderately wounded, but your fantasy ratings indicate that some more intense feelings are present. You were hurt more that you thought, or more that you were willing to admit to yourself. This may be an important awareness, which you can now work with instead of repressing or denying its effects.

Awareness of your fantasies is the first step. But how do you stop having them? That's not as easy to do. You have to work through and resolve your feelings about the injury and the person to accomplish this, but one strategy that can help begin the process is for you to engage in some self-talk in your thoughts every time you begin to think any of the fantasies, wishes, and desires about that person or event. For example, if you are longing and yearning for your parent to apologize for the hurts they inflicted, some self-talk may help. Here are some examples of such self-talk statements:

- It is unrealistic to expect that my parent will change, and wishing such a change won't make it happen.

- I cannot change another person.

- I will rise above the hurts my parent inflicted and become a better person.

- I need to accept my parent and not expect my parent to meet my expectations.

- Nothing has worked to this point, so why am I expecting it to work now?

- I don't need to hurt my parent in order for me to feel better.

- I'll love, accept, and approve of my essential inner self.

- I have got more constructive and satisfying things to do than to wish for the improbable from my parent.

You will need to continue to work on giving up your fantasies. They will not disappear simply because you think you have decided to give them up; they will continue to persist in your nonconscious and unconscious, lurking undetected. Don't become impatient with yourself when you find that you still have some fantasies. Just say to yourself that you have more work to do, the hurt was deeper than you thought, and that you will overcome it at some point.

Now let's turn to some self-building strategies that will also reduce your need for these fantasies.

Strategy 2: Negative and Positive Self-Statements

Your self-absorbed parent is probably adept at triggering your insecurities, your negative thoughts about your essential inner self, your feelings of inadequacy, and so on. Another contributor to the trigger may be your current self-statements, which may be generally inaccurate, unrealistic, illogical, and negative. You can short-circuit this process by realizing when your thoughts and feelings are responses to negative self-statements, and substituting positive self-statements. Here are some possible positive self-statements to counter typical negative self-statements. You can also develop your own positive self-statements.

Negative self-statement: The criticism is correct.

Positive self-statement: I have many strengths and talents.

Negative self-statement: I should attend to others' demands and expectations for me even if I think they are unrealistic.

Positive self-statement: I can decide for myself what I should do, and don't have to give in to others' demands and expectations.

Negative self-statement: I must always meet others' expectations even when these are too high, unrealistic, or demanding.

Positive self-statement: I do meet many expectations held by others, but don't have to meet all of them.

Negative self-statement: I'm searching for external affirmation of my worth.

Positive self-statement: I can value and cherish my essential inner self without requiring external validation.

Negative self-statement: I'm supposed to control everything.

Positive self-statement: I am able to handle and resolve most situations.

Negative self-statement: I'm supposed to keep others from feeling distress.

Positive self-statement: I can care about others without "catching" their feelings.

Negative self-statement: I should be perfect.

Positive self-statement: I have many strengths, and I am working on what I perceive as flaws.

Negative self-statement: I should never make mistakes.

Positive self-statement: I am able to learn from my mistakes.

Negative self-statement: If I were better, I'd have better relationships.

Positive self-statement: I'm good enough, and can form meaningful relationships.

Negative self-statement: I'm supposed to take on others' feelings, and take care of them.

Positive self-statement: My boundaries can be strong so that I can care for others without becoming enmeshed or overwhelmed, and recognize the limits of my responsibility for others' welfare.

Strategy 3: Altruism

Altruism is a gift to others that is free from obligations, expectations, demands, reciprocity, or any strings attached. You give freely not because you are forced, shamed, or guilty, or for your own satisfaction. You give because you want the other person to have whatever it is. Gifts can be tangible or intangible.

The few studies done on altruism have all pointed out the beneficial effects for the giver. Yes, the receiver gets the gift, but the giver also receives positive outcomes, even when the receiver does not know the giver. So you can bestow a gift without the receiver's knowledge and still receive the benefits from your altruism.

The saying about performing "random acts of kindness" suggests a way to be altruistic. You will be giving an unexpected gift of kindness without any strings attached, and that is altruistic. You may think of yourself as a kind person, and you probably are, but only when you think about it, or for certain people, or just in those instances where you expect to reap some benefit or reward. In other words, you choose where to bestow your kindness. Altruism would be when you do kind acts for anyone, and you do not expect anything for yourself to result from what you do.

In order to understand altruism, let's contrast it with acts and attitudes that may be good or helpful (or not), but are not altruistic. Such acts and attitudes include the following:

- Reminding others to say "Thank you" is an expectation and a demand.

- Wanting or needing expressions of appreciation.

- Doing something to gain attention or admiration.

- Asking people if they like what you gave them or what you did for them shows that you need their approval.

- Reminding people of what you did for them, or what you gave them.

- Expecting something in return for what you do, or for what you give.

- Using "gifts" to manipulate people or to form alliances.

- Trying to "buy" your way into someone's affections.

- Bragging or boasting about what you did for someone, or what you gave them.

- Becoming angry or upset when you feel your "gift" was not appreciated, or not appreciated enough.

As you can see, these are not acts or attitudes that are free from demands, expectations, or strings.

You may wonder what you can do or say that would be altruistic. You first have to tell yourself that your actions are without strings, they will be freely given. Second, you may need to remind yourself of number one from time to time. Third, you will want to derive your own set of altruistic acts, but you can begin with one or more of the following:

- Volunteer work of all kinds, such as helping a neighbor.

- Tutoring or mentoring a child.

- Visiting the elderly or shut-ins.

- Teaching a craft or skill at a community center, daycare, and the like.

- Collecting books for homeless children.

- Giving a single mother babysitting for an afternoon out.

- Cutting the grass for a sick neighbor.

- Making reading tapes for the visually impaired.

- Giving words of encouragement and support.

- Expressing your appreciation.

- Coming to someone's aid without having to be asked.

You will find that it is easy to be altruistic and the rewards are many.

Strategy 4: Reaching Out to Others

When you learn how to reach out to others without becoming enmeshed or overwhelmed, you are making significant progress in building your essential inner self. Our relations and connections with others provide significant support for our positive self-perceptions, generate good physical and emotional health, and are part of what gives meaning and purpose for our lives. Thus, there are many significant benefits for reaching out to others.

If you are reading this book, you have probably had many hurtful experiences that are giving you ample reasons to be cautious and wary about reaching out to others. It is only wise to learn from your experiences. But you may have pulled back so far that you often feel isolated and alienated. Finding your way to reach out to others can be helpful in reducing these feelings.

You may have to use some encouraging self-talk to get started. For example, you can remind yourself of your goal, and to try not to be disappointed and to try to understand others' responses rather than giving up when it appears that someone is not as responsive as you would like. Meaningful relationships usually take time to develop, and "instant intimacy" is often disappointing.

What are some possibilities for reaching out to others? Read the list provided in the above section on altruism for some ideas. These ideas can also be used as starting points for reaching out to others, but if you expect something in return, that takes it out of the altruism category. You are still being helpful, but you are also trying to make a connection to benefit yourself.

Let's say that you initiate contact in an effort to reach out. Where do you go from there? Try some or all of the following:

- Show interest in the other person and try to talk about them and not about you.

- Listen to them more often than you talk about your own concerns.

- Find something to appreciate about each person and be willing to communicate this to that person.

- Respect the other person's psychological boundaries and make sure that yours are also respected.

- Don't rush to solve others' problems or concerns. Show confidence in their ability to take care of whatever is needed.

- Don't try to take over others' lives, and don't let your life be taken over.

- Acknowledge and respect differences of opinion, values, and thoughts.

- Find mutual interests and activities with another person, and participate in these.

Reaching out to others does not mean that you will never again experience wounding. You may, but if you are building your essential inner self at the same time, the wounding will be mild and you will be more easily able to soothe it, fix it, or let go of it. This is part of your overall goal to heal past wounding and to minimize current and future wounding.

Strategy 5: Beauty and Wonder

Beauty cannot be defined because the perception of what is beautiful is individualistic. Different people find different things to be beautiful, and what seems beautiful to one person may not seem beautiful to someone else. *Wonder* is also individualistic and is the childlike quality of noticing some-thing new and novel, being curious about it, and deriving excitement and interest from it. It's like when a child discovers something for the first time and becomes thrilled, fascinated, and intrigued.

Beauty and wonder are discussed here because they can be enriching, and that which enriches us and our lives is construc-tive. These are added dimensions that expand our conscious-ness of our world and of our selves. They help to expand and enhance the ordinary, mundane, or even depressing things in life, and that can lead to inspiration or the spiritual.

Although the perception of beauty can vary from person to person, let's focus on what you find beautiful. Try the following. Notice the beauty around you at this moment and make a pledge to yourself to see something of beauty every day. Doing so is another way to nourish and refresh your self. Too often you may be focused so much on things you cannot change, problems you cannot solve, and planning for the future to notice beauty in your world. Pay more attention and seek out the beauty that comes your way.

Another enriching experience will be to expand your concept of beauty to include new things. You may want to con-sider things like some of the following to determine if they could fit into your definition for beauty.

- Smiles and other pleasant facial expressions

- A summer, spring, fall, or winter day

- Scenery, such as a mountain, desert, or beach

- Children at play

- A well-constructed phrase, sentence, or book

- Music other than your favorite kind

- Moving performances, such as athletic or dramatic

The world is full of beauty; we just have to be open to see it.

Wonder is also all around us if you have a sense of humor, curiosity, interest, and are open to learning new things. When you look at something in a new way, it is different and you've learned something about it. Wonder is a characteristic that inventors, scientists, scholars, and others who invent or discover knowledge have. Children have an abundant supply. For them, everything they encounter for the first time is a source for wonder, and it often continues to be so even when they've seen it many times before. This is one of the reasons that they ask so many what and why questions.

If you cannot recapture some delight, interest, or pleasure from doing some of the

things you previously did, or the new ones you developed, you may be depressed. In fact, this is one of the symptoms of depression. Although the depression may be mild or situational, it could be helpful to get medical and therapeutic assistance before it becomes deeper and more enduring.

You may feel that you are too mature to enjoy doing things you did as you grew up, or you may be physically unable, or have other constraints. This does not have to limit your search for wonder. You can develop new interests and curiosity. These come from within and are under your control. People get ideas from noticing things all around them every day. They wonder about many things and ask questions like the following:

How does that work?

Why does this happen?

How did she do that?

What would happen if?

Can I find out ----------?

What would make this better?

What can I do that would be helpful?

What's in this?

Why do they do that?

If you have a sense of wonder, you can always find something of interest; you are never bored and are continuing to grow and develop in constructive ways.

Strategy 6: Change of Pace

Routine can be comforting because it is known and consistent. You do not have to be alert, careful, or think about possibilities. People who grew up in homes lacking in routine may be edgy, tense, always on guard; they tend to expect problems, and have a variety of physical and psychological concerns. Disorganization, chaos, unpredictability, and unreliability can be very upsetting, especially if they are a part of your regular life. They can make you long for routine, consistency, and predictability where you can rest, relax, and become calm.

However, you can also become so stuck in routines that you limit yourself, become afraid to expand your horizons, to meet new people or challenges, or to learn and develop your resources and talents. In this way you place constraints on your essential self and limit your growth and development. An occasional change of pace can energize you and your thoughts in many ways, enrich your inner self, and provide for wonder and beauty in your life.

This is not to say that you should disrupt your life and do away with your routines. Some routines are beneficial. For example, I do my writing in the morning shortly after I wake up. I first read the paper and have a cup of coffee. After that I pick up my pad and pen and begin to write. Yes, I'm still in the dark ages of writing with a pad and pen. They go almost everywhere with me and are readily available, unlike my computer. This works for me. It seems to be a constructive routine for me, and I will keep it as long as I continue to be productive. You too will want to retain your constructive routines. Change of pace is not a major disruption, it is doing something different on a trial basis to see if it is right for you, if it is energizing in some way, or if that change has other positive outcomes. It can be almost anything that is different from your usual routine.

By now you get the idea and can come up with your own personal change-of-pace ideas. Try them, and if they don't fit or work for you, think of different ones. Just don't give up. Also, note how you feel during and after you try something different. Some things will not work for you and can be discarded. This is valuable information. You now know what to do. A change of pace can be rewarding, but you don't want to have constant change, as that can be stressful. Just enough change, every so often and under your control, can bring about desirable results.

Strategy 7: Mindfulness

Becoming mindful teaches you valuable concentration that can help you stay focused on what is important. This can be very helpful to you in interactions with your self-absorbed parent, where your heightened emotional state can be distracting. Once you get distracted or lost, your parent can gain the advantage and once again you leave with the same old feelings.

Mindfulness is done with conscious thought and intention. You expand your awareness in the moment, you notice, appreciate, and sometimes even savor what you are experiencing. This awareness enables you to notice things you did not notice before, to bring something into clearer focus, to sort through confusing stimuli and zone in on important aspects. It can reduce some of your anxiety and let you feel more in control. For example, let's suppose that you have practiced mindfulness as described later, and have become somewhat comfortable and proficient at using it. You decide to try to be more mindful in the next interaction with your self-absorbed parent. You might experience the following:

- You notice that your parent is showing many signs of aging, some of which you don't remember seeing before.

- Your parent is saying the usual hurtful things, but you are not confused about why the parent is doing this and are able to see the fear your parent has of becoming old and no longer in control.

- The words used by your parent seem meaningless and inaccurate, and although they are designed to hurt you, they are now bouncing around harmlessly like ball bearings.

- You are able to discern your parent's anxiety without taking it on your essential inner self, or even feeling that you must fix it.

- You are becoming aware that a role shift is in process, that your parent is fighting it, but is also unaware of it.

- You leave the interaction less upset and stressed than usual.

Mindfulness allows you to both expand and contract. You expand your awareness and contract your focus. Find a mindfulness activity to practice and do that until it becomes effortless.

Strategy 8: Reduce Your Own Self-Absorption

The major premise for this suggestion to reduce your own self-absorption is that self-absorbed behaviors and attitudes are not constructive or helpful. It is important to remember that, just as your self-absorbed parent cannot see their undeveloped narcissism, you may also be unaware of the behaviors and attitudes you have that are reflective of undeveloped narcissism. Your undeveloped narcissism may do the following:

- Prevent you from detoxifying yourself and developing your essential inner self.

- Reduce your ability to develop sufficient boundary strength to prevent becoming wounded by your self-absorbed parent.

- Keep you in a position where you can be easily wounded by your parent and by others.

- Interfere with developing and maintaining meaningful and satisfying relationships.

- Get in the way of your reaching out and connecting to others.

- Keep you on guard and in a defensive state most of the time.

There are many good reasons to reduce your self-absorption, and when you are able to do so you will find that you are much less toxic, have better relationships, and are more confident and self-assured. Be aware that this is a lifelong endeavor, and that although you are mostly unaware of many of your self-absorbed behaviors and attitudes, they do have a significant effect on your essential inner self and on your relationships.

Positive Revenge

Revenge is defined here as getting even, making others pay, showing that you are stronger and more powerful despite a real or imaginary injury, such as what you probably encountered with your self-absorbed parent. You were hurt and you want that person to be hurt in return. You think and feel that that person was wrong, and that the injury was intentional and directed at you. In addition, you may not have been in a position where you could prevent being injured or effectively retaliate.

Not only were you hurt, you were "made" to feel inadequate, powerless, ineffective, and shamed. You want to retaliate and make the other person hurt and be sorry for hurting you. This perspective is what I call "negative revenge," and when carried out it does not usually make you feel better. Moreover, the other person may not even notice your efforts to retaliate. In addition, retaliation might arouse your guilt as you realize that you are not living up to your personal standards.

The concept of "positive revenge" allows you to exact a different kind of revenge and to show the other person that they were wrong without compromising your own values and principles. These positive revenge strategies may not hurt the other person as you were hurt, but they are a way of presenting an "in your face" to that person. You do not have to inflict narcissistic injury in order to get even.

Let's start with you thinking about what would be more irritating to your self-absorbed parent: telling off that parent, or living well in spite of that parent's self-absorbed behaviors and attitudes that affected you. Positive revenge would be the latter, where you achieve meaningful, lasting, and satisfying relationships, enjoy your life and have meaning and purpose in it, live in a balanced and grounded way, and like and love yourself. Wouldn't having these achievements show your parent that that parent was wrong in how they treated you, that you survived and are thriving in spite of their best efforts to keep you under their control, that you are able to handle their negativity toward you, and that you are not destroyed or cowed by them? Wouldn't this be rewarding and affirming for you? In essence, the old saying of "Living well is the best revenge" can come to life when you focus on positive revenge.

The information, reflections, and activities presented in this book can assist you to do all of the things that will enrich your life as well as being a rebuttal to the injuries your self-absorbed parent inflicted. Among the strategies that you can use are the following:

- Repel negativity.

- Find your embedded strengths.

- Become good enough.

- Find joy, meaning, and purpose.

- Make your life count.

- Give your perceptions, opinions, and demands more prominence and priority.

Let's go into these strategies in a bit more detail so that you can find ways to implement them.

Repel negativity emanating from the self-absorbed parent by using your emotional insulation. This can also work with other people. By screening out negativity, you avoid incorporating it into your essential inner self and allowing it to erode your self-esteem. This can also help to protect you from narcissistic injuries.

Find your embedded strengths that you may be overlooking or failing to use. One way to try to identify these strengths is to list what you consider to be some weaknesses, then reflect on what embedded strength could be in that perceived weakness and work to foster its growth and development. For example, if you think a weakness is the inability to say no and to stick to it, a possible embedded strength could be your sensitivity for others' disappointment. Growing and developing that sensitivity while at the same time strengthening your commitment to be able to say no and stick to it can help you attain both goals. It is possible to be sensitive to others while not giving in to their needs and demands at the expense of yours.

Become good enough includes acceptance of your inability to always be perfect, and a realization that everything does not have to be done well, that excellence is an aspiration attainable at times, but that most of the time good enough is the best that you can do, and that that is acceptable. It's not the end of the world if you cannot be excellent at everything. That does not mean that you stop trying, it just means that you can be okay with some things as less than excellent, especially if you are also trying to be as good as possible.

Find joy, meaning, and purpose. These are the fundamentals for a rich and enjoyable life. With these you are able to live, laugh, and love, to expand your horizons, to connect to others and to the universe, and to be balanced and grounded. Are these things that your self-absorbed parent has? Would that parent be happier if they did have them? How about you? How do you think these would enrich your life?

Make your life count for something positive—your children's welfare, your intimate partner's well-being, your own health and well-being, altruistic actions, and other such positives. Counting for something does not mean attention, admiration, status, power, control, and other things like these, as they are of little value in the long run. Decide what you want for your life to mean and work to attain that.

Giving your perceptions, opinions, and demands more priority means that you stop trying to meet the impossible demands of your self-absorbed parent, and take charge of who you are and what you do. That does not mean that you become self-centered as is your parent, it means that you become self-reflective and self-caring. You do things for yourself and for others because you want to do them, not because you feel obligated to or because you feel guilty or ashamed. You are in charge of your essential inner self as much as you can be.

Summary

This chapter focused on presenting eight strategies: techniques and actions you can take to stop hurting from your self-absorbed parent's toxic-producing behaviors and attitudes. Described were some positive steps you can take to building a stronger and more resilient inner essential self and other positive outcomes. The toxic effects of your self-absorbed parent on you can be detrimental to your relationships, to your ability to think in constructive ways, and above all to improve how you feel about yourself. You are encouraged to reflect on the suggestions provided in this chapter and to create some of your own.

CHAPTER ACTIVITIES

Visualization

Sit in a quiet place where you will not be interrupted or disturbed. Close your eyes and imagine that you have become the person you want to be. Visualize how you will feel, what you will do, and how you will behave toward significant others in your life.

Writing

Make a list of your major or most troubling time-wasters that are under your control. Write a sentence about each, and list an action you could take to eliminate or at least reduce the amount of time that you find unproductive.

Draw/Collage

Draw or collage your self as a color. Materials needed will be a sheet of paper and a set of crayons or markers or colored pencils that have a selection of different hues of some colors. You can select your favorite color or another color. The many aspects of your self can be illustrated by a variation of that color. For example, if you selected blue, the aspects could range from a light blue to a midnight blue. Write the name of the aspect on the color.

CHAPTER 7

Strategies to Strengthen Your Self

Introduction

Your awareness of your own self-absorbed behaviors and attitudes is probably scant or nonexistent. That is, you do not see what you are saying, doing, believing, or thinking that conveys self-absorption. You fail to understand all of the negative impact of these behaviors and attitudes just as your parent fails to see or understand the impact of their self-absorbed behavior and attitudes. You have probably tried to bring these to the parent's attention, but the parent is unaware of them and will dismiss or deny your characterization of their behaviors and attitudes. This lack of perception can be difficult to understand, but it is real. The parent simply cannot see what you and others can see so clearly. The same blindness is true for everyone else, including you. Just as your parent does not, so too do you not see your own self-absorbed behaviors and attitudes.

The first step to reduce or eliminate self-absorbed behaviors and attitudes is to accept a hypothesis that you do have and exhibit some self-absorbed behaviors and attitudes. The second step is to say to yourself that you want to become more aware of these so that you can reduce or eliminate them. Throughout all of this, you must firmly keep in mind that this understanding takes work, that it is an unfolding process, and that behavior change takes time to develop. Patience with yourself can be helpful as you grow and develop.

After completing, or at least starting, steps one and two, it's time to move on and to identify what you want to change and where you want to grow. The previous chapters provided you with information and strategies to begin, and this chapter provides some suggestions for changing specific self-absorbed behaviors and attitudes. Although eleven behaviors and attitudes are described, that does not mean that you have all of them. However, you would want to consider if you have a mild version of each of them. The outcome will be that you develop your personal action plan, one that fits you and your circumstances. The specific categories reflecting self-absorption presented in this chapter include the following:

- Entitlement—an attitude that conveys arrogance, contempt, and superiority.

- Attention seeking—actions that ensure that you are constantly the center of attention.

- Admiration seeking—searching for external recognition, esteem, and approval.

- Grandiosity and its flip side, the impoverished self—the grand and inflated self, and the other side, the deflated self.

- Extensions of self—incomplete recognition and understanding of the boundaries that define where you end and where others begin.

- Unique and special—the excessive desire to be considered as incomparable and matchless.

- Exploitation of others—taking advantage of others for your personal benefit.

- Shallow emotions—being unable to experience or express deep emotions other than fear or anger.

- Lack of empathy—being unable to understand or to be compassionate with others' feelings.

- Emptiness—the essential core inner self is empty.

- Envy—the belief that others are less deserving and less worthy than you, and that they do not deserve what they get that you want.

Now that you are aware of these personal self-absorbed behaviors and attitudes, you can begin to reduce or even eliminate some of them.

Entitlement

An entitlement attitude is demonstrated when you feel that you are supposed to receive preferential treatment—that you should be forgiven for errors and mistakes; that you can hurt others without penalty or having to feel guilt or shame; that you can do or say whatever you want to others and they should not object; that you should receive all or most of the rewards and none of the punishments; and so on. This attitude carries with it the notion that you deserve special considerations and treatment, and that others should agree that you deserve these. It also carries with it an insensitivity to others, an unawareness that others exist and are worthwhile, and an unspoken conviction that others are aware of and accept your specialness and superiority.

Reflection: Just in case I unconsciously have and display some version of an entitlement attitude, I can reduce this by becoming more aware of the impact of my behavior on others and by questioning some assumptions I have about how others are supposed to act toward and treat me.

Attention Seeking

Attention-seeking behaviors and attitudes include the following:

- Talking loudly even when you are in a place where your talking will disturb others.

- Making grand entrances and exits so that you will be noticed by everyone.

- Dressing flamboyantly or in a manner to emphasize your sexuality.

- Doing something to distract or "upstage" another person who has the spotlight at that moment.

- Starting a (verbal) fight.

- Interrupting an ongoing conversation.

- Dropping hints and teasers.

The intent of these kinds of behaviors is to gain outside validation that you are significant, important, different, and better than others, and to reassure yourself that you do indeed exist and are worthwhile. Without attention, self-doubt begins to emerge, you become anxious and maybe even afraid, and this discomfort impels you to act.

Reflection: Can I try to validate myself and reduce my need for external validation? I can become more aware of my attention-seeking behaviors, such as talking loudly, and reduce such behaviors.

Admiration Seeking

Admiration seeking refers to the need and yearning for reassurance that you are superior and valued. Behaviors such as boasting, bragging, and fishing for compliments are examples of admiration seeking. Other examples include thinking and feeling that you deserve to be recognized for any of the following:

- Being more deserving than others.

- Having talent and ability.

- Owning more possessions or more costly ones than others.

- Achieving and accomplishing.

- Your family or other connections (status).

These are just a few examples. It is not so much that these are not laudatory things that can and do bring admiration, but that it is not helpful or constructive if the person seeks to do or focus on them just to gain the admiration of others. Pride in yourself and your accomplishments is appropriate and uplifting. But admiration seeking goes beyond this kind of inner pride to actively seeking and demanding approval, compliments, and even envy from others. That is a self-absorbed behavior that can be reduced or even eliminated.

Reflection: I can compliment myself and refrain from boasting and bragging. If I truly believe that I accomplished something wonderful, that can be enough, and I don't have to have external validation.

Grandiosity

The subtle signs of grandiosity are those that unconsciously reveal an inflated and unrealistic perception of one's self. People who are grandiose, or who have some grandiosity, are unaware of what is being revealed, and even if this is pointed out to them they are unlikely to accept that perception. This is indeed an overvaluing of oneself, a feeling of superiority, and an expansiveness that does not recognize limitation or boundaries. I am not talking only about the signs of grandiosity that are evident and obvious, but also about the thoughts and ideas that seem reasonable to that person on the surface but that in reality are unrealistic, illogical, and irrational. Some examples of this subtle grandiosity are the following:

- Walking in and immediately taking over the conversation or whatever is being done.

- Taking on an excessive number of responsibilities, such as the inability to say no when you are already overcommitted.

- The attitude that what you do is better than what others do.

- Superman/Superwoman.

- Arrogance.

- Contempt for others, and feeling that they are inferior.

- Being unable to see merit in anyone else's ideas or opinions.

- Having to "have" or to "do" it all.

You may think that you do not have any undiscovered grandiosity, but it is likely that you are refusing to notice it.

Reflection: Review the list above and be truthful with yourself about your behavior and attitudes that are reflective of grandiosity. Remind yourself of these when you find that your thinking and attitudes are such as these and make a conscious effort to do something different at that moment. Implementing some of the other growth and development strategies can help to reduce your grandiosity.

The Impoverished Self

The impoverished self is the essential inner self that feels deprived, ignored, neglected, not nurtured or treated fairly. The important point is how you feel, not what is real. For example, you could be deprived but not feel that you are deprived. Or you could be in a position where you were not being nurtured, but not have a sense of having missed anything.

Let's suppose that in fact many of these states are real for you, that is, you are being treated unfairly and you are being ignored. Instead of bemoaning these facts and feeling that you must be unworthy to have to experience these, it would be more helpful and constructive if you could focus on your strengths, turn your thoughts and energies to something more positive in your life, take steps to make changes that will get you treated fairly and bring you the recognition you deserve, and so on. You don't have to stay mired in your misery.

Reflection: Have you been accused of complaining a lot, even when you think you are just talking about your circumstances and don't see this as complaining? Is it possible that you whine, mope, kvetch, and so on? Are you more focused on what is wrong or miserable about your situation than on what is positive and pleasant? You may want to try the following: Every day for a month, write three pleasant or positive things that you encountered, saw, felt, or experienced that day. At the end of the month, review these writings and take stock of your feelings.

Lack of Empathy

Lack of empathy is a very self-absorbed behavior and attitude that has a serious negative impact on your relationships. Empathy is sensing and feeling at a deep level what the other person is experiencing. You do not just hear the words, you feel and understand at a deeper level the meaning behind the words. Listening to content can be important, but the real message is located in the feelings of the speaker (sender), and your ability to be empathic determines if you are able to hear the real message behind the words. People who have not yet developed their capacity to be empathic can find that they often have difficult relationships, including their intimate relationships.

Let's back up a little and note that you cannot be empathic with everyone all of the time. Even gifted and highly experienced clinicians cannot do this. Further, it can be dangerous sometimes to be open to receiving feelings from others, especially if you are emotionally susceptible or lack sufficient psychological boundary strength. However, since you are an adult with at least some degree of healthy self-reflection, you are probably capable of being empathic with many people some of the time. This topic is discussed in more detail in the next chapter.

Reflection: Do I really focus on and listen to others, or do I tend to let my attention and thoughts wander to other things, such as what I intend to say as a response? Do I listen for other people's feelings behind their words, or am I more focused on what I am feeling?

Extensions of Self

Self-absorbed people are only dimly aware of other people in the world as separate and distinct from them, and at the unconscious level they think that others exist to serve them. This belief is very much like that which infants and children have, but it is being acted on by an adult. These self-absorbed people see everything in terms of their self, as if they were the only real people in the world and others were only shadows to be ordered around.

This unconscious attitude is also a part of the explanation for why these people do not respect other people's boundaries.

They don't see or expect such boundaries because they see everyone else as dependent on them and under their control, and they believe that they should be allowed to do or say whatever they want to without any objection. Some acts that reflect this attitude include the following:

- Borrowing or taking others' possessions without their permission.

- Making social or other arrangements without consultation with other family members.

- Making choices and discussions for other people who are able to choose and decide for themselves.

- Entering other people's rooms or offices without knocking first and waiting for an invitation to enter.

- Touching someone without asking permission (children and pregnant women get this a lot).

- Asking personal questions, such as how much did that cost, when are you getting married, why don't you have children, and so on.

Reflection: Do I consciously or unconsciously violate others' boundaries? Am I always respectful of the other person's privacy, space, and so on? I need to become more aware of when I may violate others' boundaries, as well as when my own boundaries are violated.

Unique and Special

Everyone wants to be appreciated as a unique, special, and worthwhile person. However, self-absorbed people take this desire to an extreme and demand that everyone respond to them as if they were significantly superior to everyone else in the world. Such people think that their work, their productions, their talent, or their very existence is so far superior to that of others that other people can never hope to attain their level. Further, such people are convinced that it is the responsibility of all other people in the world to recognize this specialness, and to be admiring and deferential. The self-absorption of such people can blind them to respecting the rights of others, or even to recognizing that others too are worthwhile and unique. Some behaviors and attitudes reflective of this characteristic include the following:

- Self-aggrandizing comments and remarks.

- Constantly pointing out others' faults and flaws.

- Frequently speaking of what others should and ought to be and do.

- Comparing other people unfavorably to oneself.

- Blaming others for getting in one's way.

- Commenting on how the person does everything better.

- Expecting to be chosen, complimented, and recognized for achievements before anyone else.

Self-absorbed people have an underdeveloped appreciation for others, think that they are the only unique and special people in the world, and are unaware of their self-absorbed behaviors and attitudes and of the impact of these on others.

Reflection: I know that I am unique and special, but I wonder if I am fully aware that others are also unique and special? Do I constantly promote myself and fail to recognize others' accomplishments? How can I become more aware of what I am doing, saying, and believing?

Exploitation

Using others to gain personal benefits is exploitation. Coupled with this is the attitude and conviction that others are not worthy, that they exist to serve the exploiter, and that they are inferior to the exploiter. While people with a DNP exploit everyone in some way, the people closest to them are the ones who suffer the most because the relationship is used to promote and support the exploitation. The self-absorbed person is capitalizing on others' caring, concern, good nature, desire to please, need for approval, and other such personality factors. This is done to meet the personal needs of the person with the DNP, and to the detriment of other people. What are some exploitive acts?

- Borrowing money but not paying it back.

- Expecting favors for oneself but not reciprocating.

- Urging, cajoling, or persuading someone to do something that is not in that person's best interests, but that is something where the self-absorbed person gains.

- Lying, cheating, distorting, and misleading to gain an advantage.

- Using "If you loved me" or "If you cared about me" to get others to do something they do not want to do.

There are many other exploitive acts, and you can probably add to the list, especially if you have a self-absorbed parent. Does (did) your parent do the following?

- Expect you to drop what you are doing to do something for them.

- Have an expectation that you will make the parent's wants and needs your highest priority.

- Blame you for the parent's discomfort or misery.

- Use guilt or shame to manipulate you to do things you do not want to do.

- Criticize you for not reading the parent's mind and giving or doing what they want or need.

- Expect you to live up to the parent's vision of themselves.

Now let's turn those behaviors and attitudes around to get an idea of how you may be exploiting others. I know you do not believe that you are doing this, but you may not be aware of these behaviors and attitudes in your essential inner self. Look at all the items in both lists, and reflect on what you do and say in your closest family, work, social, or intimate relationships that are similar to those in the list. These are the behaviors and attitudes you can work to change.

Reflection: How much do I like to be able to do better than others, and what am I willing to do to ensure that I come out on top, or as a winner? Do I unintentionally exploit relationships for my gain? Do I try to get people to do things for me just because I want them to? Am I sensitive to the potential I may have for exploiting my relationships?

Shallow Emotions

Adults with healthy narcissism can experience and express a wide and deep variety of emotions. In contrast, self-absorbed adults are extremely limited in experiencing and expressing their feelings. Experiencing for them seems to be mainly limited to fear and anger, and while they have the words when expressing other feelings, they don't have the accompanying emotions. These people are not genuine in their expression of feelings, except for the variations of fear and anger.

Reflection: Think about the feelings you have experienced so far today. Did you do any of the following?

- *Expressed few feelings openly and directly, and most of those were negative.*

- *Communicated only a few feelings, either positive or negative, to someone.*

- *You had very few feelings or did not have any intense feelings.*

- *You have a very short feeling vocabulary list of words.*

Ask yourself if you may be too focused on negative feelings, whether you want to increase the number of positive feelings you experience and express, and whether you need to develop a larger vocabulary of feeling words.

Emptiness

This state is difficult to describe because empty is usually defined as the absence of something, and as having borders, as for example around a hole. The psychological state of emptiness is also an absence, but without borders or defining points, and that makes it even more difficult to describe. There is nothing. The following description does not fully capture the emptiness of self-absorbed people, but it does provide some descriptors.

The core of the self is empty, and some or all of the following qualities are *lacking*:

- Meaningful connection to others.

- Connection to the universe (inspiration or spirituality).

- Capacity for varied and deep feelings.

- An understanding of what others are experiencing.

- Compassion and mercy.

- Appreciation for beauty and wonder.

- Self as separate and distinct, having value and worth.

- Capacity for loving and cherishing oneself and others.

- Transcending oneself for others.

The empty person does not know any other state and assumes that others have the same empty core. No one outside the person can provide what is lacking. That has to come from within, and that person may not realize what is lacking or feel a need to fill the void.

Many people who do not have a DNP may have some voids at the core of self. However, they recognize what is lacking and take steps to try to get what is needed. People with a DNP are completely, or almost completely, empty at the core; they can sense a lack but cannot identify what is lacking. They think that others have something they do not, and they try to get it, but they fail because they do not know what they are trying to get. Instead of reflection and growing the self, some people substitute activity. Other substitutions include the following:

- Substance abuse.

- Blind allegiance to a "calling," such as a cult, religion, or charismatic person.

- Gambling.

- Overeating or undereating.

- Shopping and overspending.

- Overly committing your time and effort to civic, social, and other such activities.

The void is never filled, and they continue to try to find something to combat the emptiness.

Since almost everyone can have some lacks or holes, what prevents and overcomes emptiness?

- Meaningful, satisfying, and enduring relationships.

- Meaning and purpose for one's life.

- A rich and satisfying inspirational aspect of life.

- Reaching out and touching others to enrich their lives.

- Expanding the self to be creative, empathic, and wise.

Reflection: Am I aware of my holes? Am I using constructive means to fill these, or am I relying on unconstructive actions? What can I do to enrich my life?

Envy

Let's define envy as wanting what someone else has and also feeling that you are more deserving of it than they are. Both are the components of envy, but it is the second component that is the most corrosive. Wanting something can be motivating and a challenge to try to get whatever is wanted. For example, if you want a promotion you can work hard and do the things necessary to achieve the promotion. Or if you want wealth, then you can seek out ways to accumulate it. Relationships can be built, success defined and achieved, skills developed, and goals defined if you are motivated to get what you want. These are all positive and, in most cases, they may be doable.

However, if this wanting is accompanied with resentment that another person has what you want, but you feel that they are less deserving or undeserving and that somehow they did you out of something that is rightfully yours, that is when you move from just wanting something to the negative state of envy. Worse is that if you do not work to get what you want, your time and energy are now wasted on resenting the person, thinking about how you were unfairly treated, or how you can get others to see that person as you do as being undeserving and unworthy, instead of working to get what you want. This resentment and these feelings of unfair treatment are very corrosive to your self-esteem and spirit.

Even if we were to suppose that you are correct and that you are more deserving and worthy, that would not help you get what was wanted, which is the goal. Nor would the resentment and feelings of unfair treatment help in any way, because you are doing those negative things to yourself. The other people are not doing anything negative to you by having what you want, whether they are deserving or not. You are allowing the negative impacts to deflect you from achieving your successes.

Reflection: What do you have now that you would be willing to give up to get what the person you envy has? For example, if you are envious of the other person's receiving a promotion that you would have liked to have, would you be willing to give up a big part of your family or leisure time to get the promotion? How would your relationships suffer?

Goals to Become Less Self-Absorbed

It can be helpful to visualize and articulate some goals for changing your self-absorbed behavior and attitudes to some that are self-reflective instead. Self-reflective means here that you think, act, and feel in accord with what is sufficient for you, but you are also able to judge and act to put other people's well-being ahead of yours when you judge it to be necessary. You don't sacrifice your essential inner self for others, but you do give of yourself when their need is greater than yours, and you consciously decide to do so. You take care of your essential inner self, adequately protect it, and are able to reach out to others. You cease an unconscious belief that you are the center of everything and that everything else revolves around you. You reduce your actions that reflect self-absorption, and you increase your actions that reflect your awareness of others as persons who are worthwhile, unique, separate, and distinct from you.

Following are some possible goals and suggestions for changes in behavior. Change your behavior and you tend to change your attitude. Try and visualize what you will do and say that lets you know you've reached your goal for reducing or eliminating a possible self-absorbed behavior and attitude. Remember that if you do have a particular self-absorbed behavior or attitude, you are probably not consciously aware of it. That's why it is important for you to carefully consider all of the suggestions.

Self-Absorbed Characteristic	Suggestions for Changes
An entitlement attitude	Wait your turn. Do not give orders or demands. Don't expect others to do for you what you can do for yourself. Do not seek unearned credit.
Attention seeking	Let the attention come to you. Make quiet entrances and exits. Do not interrupt others. If you tend to talk loudly, try to speak quietly.
Admiration seeking	Focus on internal pleasure for your qualities and accomplishments. Cease boasting and bragging. Let compliments come to you, do not fish for them. Do not always have a personal story to tell.

Self-Absorbed Characteristic	Suggestions for Changes
Grandiosity	Recognize and accept your personal limitations, learn to say no and stick to it, reflect on a need to be superior and reduce or eliminate it.
Impoverished self	Resolve to stop complaining and whining and to act on things that can be changed or resolved. Let go of fretting over things that cannot be changed or resolved.
Lack of empathy	Increase your ability to be empathic. Stop talking and listen. Focus on the speaker. Try to hear the feelings and meaning behind the speaker's words.
Extensions of self	Develop strong and resilient boundaries. Respect others' rights and space. Do not ask favors or only ask when needed. Do not expect others to follow your orders. Make requests instead of orders or demands.
Shallow emotions	Develop a list of feeling words and try to use a new one each day. Stop periodically and reflect on what you are experiencing at that moment and try to name a feeling.
Unique and special	Appreciate others' contributions. Recognize that others too are special.
Exploitation	Become more independent, return favors, treat others fairly, don't lie, cheat, distort, or mislead.
Emptiness	Complete the related exercises in this book, perform altruistic acts, reflect on your "holes" that may exist.

Beyond Self-absorption: Meaning and Purpose

Once you are on your way to reducing your self-absorption and building healthy adult narcissism (including self-reflection), you will also want to develop more meaning and purpose in your life. Meaning and purpose expand the richness of our lives, connect us to the wider universe, and help us enjoy life. There are many positive benefits that can follow, such as reducing or eliminating isolation and alienation, combating despair, hopelessness, and helplessness, accepting oneself, obtaining more realistic expectations of yourself and others, knowing the limits of your personal responsibility, and becoming more centered and grounded.

You may want to take some time to reflect on the extent to which you are aware of the aspects of your life that can have meaning and purpose for you; where you are satisfied or pleased and where you are dissatisfied or displeased; and how you can take action to become more satisfied with your life and its meaning and purpose. You can also work to have a clearer vision of what and how you want your life to be and can visualize how you can achieve it. We now turn to describing the benefits of embarking on this work.

Isolation and Alienation

This refers to a psychological and emotional distancing of yourself from others; feeling disconnected and alone; lacking direction, meaning, and purpose in your life; and not being able to see how you can effect positive changes. Although this description may sound like depression, it does not have the clinical and physical aspects of depression. This is an existential dilemma that everyone can experience off and on throughout their lives. It has no definitive answer, only momentary ones, and can emerge where your life's meaning and purpose are not to your satisfaction.

Feeling isolated or alienated is like being adrift in the universe with no reference points, such as the following, for locating yourself:

- Meaningful and satisfying relationships.

- Enjoyment, pleasure, and delight.

- A sense of being wanted and needed.

- Seeing that your contributions are appreciated and helpful.

- Feeling competent and effective in many aspects of your life.

When one or more of these reference points are missing, you may begin to feel alone and cut off from other people. These feelings can intensify until they become feelings of being isolated and alienated.

Despair, Helplessness, and Hopelessness

Milder versions of despair include discouragement and dejection. Minor versions of helplessness include ineffectuality and impotence. Minor versions of hopelessness include feeling that things are impossible or bleak. I mention these because you may not have the intense version for these feelings but may not be aware that you are experiencing some of the milder versions. These too can contribute to lack of or reduced meaning and purpose for your life.

Despair, helplessness, and hopelessness refer to your perception of your effectiveness in your life and your ability to control what you think of as being under your control. This last perception is the one that may be fueling your discouragement, dejection, or despair. You may want to refer back to the discussion about extensions of self at this point, for that can be contributing to your perceptions about the extent of your control; that is where you think that other people are, or should be, under your control. When they don't do what you want them to, this can make you feel ineffectual. You fail to accept that they were not under your control, that they are not under your control, and that they will never be under your control. You have an unrealistic expectation, some underdeveloped narcissism that needs work so that you more fully understand and accept at both a conscious and unconscious level that others are separate and distinct from you, and then you can give up the fantasy that others should do what you want them to do.

There are many uncontrollable things in life, such as the economy, your talents and ability, what other people say and do, and so on. Some things are just too large and complex to be under anyone's control—wars, for example. You must develop a realistic perception of what is and what is not under your control. This change will not prevent you from feeling discouraged, but it will prevent you from feeling despair, helpless, and hopeless. However, you will have to give up fantasies that you have power and control over any of the following:

- Making someone love you.

- Causing others to change.

- Expecting the world to always be fair and just.

- Yearning for preferential treatment.

- Controlling what others say and do.

- Thinking of your essential inner self as the only one in the universe.

Acceptance of Self and Positive Changes

You may have become more aware of some previously hidden aspects of your essential inner self as you read this book and completed the exercises. There may also be some behaviors and attitudes you became aware of that could be changed, and you may have some aspect of your essential inner self where you feel embarrassed or shamed. Not to worry, everyone has this experience and can always use more growing and developing, especially to develop healthy adult narcissism.

Your challenge will be to accept your essential inner self as you are—needed changes, shame, and all. Try not to deny, minimize, rationalize, or exaggerate any aspects of your essential inner self. Above all, don't get discouraged at the amount of work you need to do, as that will retard progress. It is much more helpful to focus most of your thoughts and energies on positives, rather than dwelling obsessively on negatives.

Some self-talk can help you with your self-acceptance. You are not ignoring or excusing what you perceive to be faults and flaws, you are working with them to effect positive changes, and it is very important to have patience with yourself, and to not give up in the face of failure or setbacks. Try some or all of the following self-talk:

Thoughts and Behaviors	Self-Talk
You are less than perfect in doing something.	It was good enough.
You make a mistake.	I'll do better next time.
You fail or encounter barriers.	I'll try harder.
You think you can't or won't succeed.	I'll do the very best I am able to do.

You feel responsible for others' feelings.	I don't need to always take care of others.
You become aware of your self-absorbed behaviors and attitudes.	I am working on this and I'll overcome many of these.
You become concerned or discouraged about your progress.	I see what I have been able to do and I will continue to work on myself.

More Realistic Expectations

You may need to develop more realistic expectations for yourself, and for others. For example, you may expect perfection for yourself, and by extension, also expect it for others. These expectations are unrealistic and can lead you to:

- Blaming yourself or others when mistakes are made or something is not perfect.

- Doing and saying things that negatively affect a relationship when your expectations are not met, even when these expectations are not specified and you expect the other person to read your mind.

- Becoming shamed and displacing this onto others, including those who are near and dear to you.

- Remaining in a constant state of anxiety that you will make a mistake.

All of these can affect your health, your self-perception, and your relationships.

Expectations are generally "shoulds" and "oughts," as in insisting that others "should" do things your way when it would be perfectly reasonable to let them do things their own way, for example, loading the dishwasher in a different way than you would do it. Further, you may have an unrealistic expectation that others "ought" to know what you want or need and "ought" to meet that want or need without your having to say a word. It can be pleasing for you when this happens, but not so pleasing when it is an expectation for you.

On the other hand, it must be noted that having high expectations for yourself can be positive. Note that I said high expectations, not unrealistic ones. For example, there is nothing wrong with seeking perfection and trying hard to attain it. What is negative is when you demand it of yourself and of others (these do seem to go together in many cases), and when you cannot accept less than perfection. Since perfection is rarely if ever attained, you remain dissatisfied with yourself and with others. Your relationships suffer since others don't have your drive for perfection and can be satisfied with simply being good enough (while at same time working to improve). This latter stance or mindset does not produce blame, shame, constant anxiety, and dissatisfaction, and these are sufficient reasons to try to adopt more realistic expectations for your self and for others.

Limits for Your Personal Responsibility

If you have not internalized that there are limits to your personal responsibility, then you have not fully come to know your essential inner self as separate and distinct from others. Further, you may be unnecessarily accepting blame, experiencing shame, perceiving yourself as ineffectual, and trying to maintain control over people and events where you cannot gain control. These issues relate to your boundary strength. Resilient boundaries are desirable, but you may have soft, rigid, or spongy boundaries. My book *Whose Life Is It Anyway? When to Stop*

Taking Care of Their Feelings and Start Taking Care of Your Own (Brown, 2002) discusses this in more detail and presents strategies that can begin to help you build sufficient boundary strength.

Some examples may help to clarify how you perceive your personal responsibility:

- Do you apologize or say you did not intend to do that when someone says that you caused (made) him or her feel a particular feeling?

- Can you be assertive when someone insists that you do something you do not want to do?

- Have you violated your personal standards, ethics, or values to please another person, or because you did not want to disappoint someone?

- Do you feel bad (shamed or guilty) when another person feels uncomfortable?

- Do you put yourself out to ensure others' comfort or pleasure?

- Do you suppress your feelings or needs so that others will not be burdened?

If many or all of these fit you, then you are taking unwarranted responsibility. You don't know, accept, or recognize that there are limits to your duty and need to care for others. It's not that you don't have some responsibility to be tactful, sensitive, and understanding of others. You do, and that can strengthen relationships. However, the acts, feelings, and attitudes described above are indicators that you have gone too far in your efforts to connect, and that when you do these things you are not taking care of yourself and are not realizing sufficiently that you are not the other person. For example, you do not cause or make someone have a particular feeling; people choose to feel a particular way for a variety of reasons that are not under your control. Yes, something in their environment may trigger their feeling, but it remains their feeling, not your responsibility.

Becoming Centered and Grounded

This chapter has focused on reducing self-absorption and describing what benefits you can gain from your continuing self-development. All of these, and some others benefits that are described in the next chapter, can lead to your becoming more centered and grounded. Doing so can help you in many ways:

- You don't lose your way and go off and do things that are not constructive and beneficial to a meaningful and purposeful life, or to your well-being.

- You choose to act in accordance with your values, and can resist manipulation by others.

- You do not fly apart, melt down, or become isolated during troubling times or in crises.

- You are able to maintain your sense of your essential inner self under very trying and distressful circumstances.

- You are able to tolerate being alone without feeling lonely.

- You choose relationships that are mutually beneficial.

- You build on your strength, and work on what you want to change about your self.

- You are able to resist becoming mired in despair, hopelessness, and helplessness.

When you are centered and grounded, you are able to encounter and experience life vicissitudes with some confidence that you will survive. You'll do the best you can and are assured that what you do, and what you are, are good enough even when you don't succeed to the extent you wanted to. You are comfortable with your essential inner self, you like yourself, you are able to accept your imperfections without feeling that they are shameful and must be hidden at all costs, and you are able to let others manage and control their own lives, thoughts, and feelings. Becoming centered and grounded has a lot of positive effects on you and on your life.

Becoming centered and grounded will also help prevent you from becoming narcissistically wounded, at least most of the time. You will always have a little more personal growing and developing to do, and nothing will entirely prevent you from being wounded, but you can reduce your vulnerability by building your self and developing healthy adult narcissism and strong and resilient boundaries. Further, you will find that it becomes easier to do the following:

- Let go of resentment and grudges.

- Stop incorporating and identifying with others' projections (projective identification).

- Accept and tolerate differences of others.

- Initiate and maintain meaningful and satisfying relationships.

- Have a meaningful and purposeful life.

The next chapter provides suggestions and strategies that are designed to promote your personal growth and development so that you can let go of even more painful events, and can move farther in getting over what has been festering for some time. You've probably let go of some hurt, resentment, and grudges from other past experiences, but maybe not all of them. You may also have reduced or eliminated your feelings about these experiences, and some negative effects that lingered. This is considerable progress and you can compliment yourself for your efforts and achievements. There is more to do, but you are really on your way!

CHAPTER ACTIVITIES

Writing

Describe in a short essay the components for a happy day for you in as much detail as possible.

Drawing/Collage

Materials: A sheet of paper and a set of crayons or felt markers or colored pencils.

Use the materials to draw the concept of happiness. This can be abstract, such as just happy colors, or representational.

Visualization

Sit in silence, close your eyes, and allow an image of happiness to emerge.

CHAPTER 8

My Ideal Self: Determine the Person You Want to Be

Introduction

Instantaneous change is possible, but not very probable, since you are a complex person with many facets of your essential inner self, some of which are unknown to you. Trying to make major changes all at once is probably not a good idea since success at all of them is unlikely, and that can be discouraging. What is proposed here is that you first try to make small changes over time. As you become more aware of your thoughts, attitudes, behaviors, self-absorption, strengths and weaknesses, boundary strength, and the extent of your narcissistic wounding, your changes can expand at an even greater rate.

The remainder of this chapter will present strategies for changes that can fortify your essential inner self and make it less vulnerable to becoming wounded by your self-absorbed parent. You've received some suggestions throughout the book, and here are even more. Some may not fit or be feasible for you, and it is not reasonable for you to use these. Go with the suggestions that make sense to you at this time. Later, after you've tried these, you can return to those you put aside and see if they can now be of use. Presented are six categories for suggested shifts: building awareness, reducing self-absorption, increasing self-reflection, cultivating your strengths, building strong and resilient boundaries, and becoming your own person.

Perceptual Shift: Building Awareness

Building awareness has already begun by your completing some or all of the activities in the previous chapters of this book. You are probably much more attuned to what you are experiencing at a given moment, how your family-of-origin and past experiences influenced who you are and how you think and feel, the extent of your psychological boundary strength and resilience, and maybe even some of your underdeveloped narcissism. You have explored what gives meaning and purpose to your life and other positive attributes that can help keep you centered and grounded. These are major accomplishments. However, there is more that can be done to help you become the kind of person you envision.

Aware people are or seek to be fully functioning humans who are mindful of the transitory nature of life, and who are also mindful of the following:

- They have an appreciation of the present.

- They have connections to the universe.

- They have an ability to see the wonder and beauty in the world.

- They listen to the messages their body sends.

- They can be fully emotionally present when listening to others.

- Their mind and body respond in symmetry, without dissonance.

- They openly and freely choose their standards, principles, and values.

- They can accept reality.

- They are able to access their feelings and identify these.

Appreciation of the present helps you to more fully be in the "now" of your existence. The past is important, it influences your present functioning and well-being, but you should also understand that your past is not necessarily relevant to the here-and-now of your everyday life. The future is unknown and uncertain, and how much it will be experienced is a guess at best, so that speculation about it is futile and can detract from the full experience of the here-and-now.

Reflection: What are you aware of right now, physically, emotionally, and psychologically?

Being a part of the universe means feeling connected, less isolated and alone, a part of something larger than yourself, and having the capacity to love and to be loved. You feel that you have some impact and influence and that you are not totally at the mercy of forces that you cannot see, understand, or control. The vastness of the universe is daunting, but not threatening. There is much to discover.

Reflection: Do you meditate or pray? How do you connect to something outside of yourself? How do you refresh your spirit?

Ability to see wonder and beauty in the world is a focus on the promise in your world, not the negativity. It is easy to get caught up in the unfairness of people and situations, to feel helpless and powerless to effectively deal with adversity, and to begin to feel hopeless and despairing. These negatives are easy to find. What is harder to focus on are the positives, such as wonder and beauty. Try to look around you and notice wonder and beauty every day.

Reflection: Take a moment to look around your immediate environment. What can you see or hear that you find beautiful or pleasing, such as something in your favorite color? What triggers your curiosity? Or perhaps you start to wonder about something.

Listening to the messages your body sends helps you to stay centered and grounded and to better understand your inner world. You can know what reactions you are having, and have some understanding of why you are reacting as you do, the influences of your past, and your personality, and you can be accepting of these even as you are trying to change some things about your essential inner self.

Reflection: What messages is your body trying to communicate to you at this time? Check out the tension, discomfort, where you feel good, parts that seem to be working right or as they should, parts that need attention such as, hunger, thirst, or being sleepy.

Being fully emotionally present when listening to others, without being distracted by inner or external concerns, enables you to hear the overt and hidden messages in the communication, to connect with the person in a meaningful way, and to better understand what that person is experiencing. You are not asking questions instead of responding empathically, you are not distracted with your thoughts of other matters, you do not change the topic, or do anything but bring your thoughts and feelings to listening to the other person.

Reflection: Can or do you screen out distractions, orient your body to the person, and turn off or ignore electronic devices? These actions can help you be more emotionally present with others.

The mind and the body respond in unison and both stay in touch with each other. The mind is not doing one thing while the body does something else. This symmetry contributes to mindfulness and awareness.

Reflection: Can you recall a time when you acted without thinking, such as putting too much salt on a dish, or forgetting to add sugar to a recipe?

Choose your own values, standards, and principles instead of acting on the basis of what you were "taught" or what others find to be of importance and have imposed. This is not to say that standards and principles from the past should be discarded. In fact, these can be kept, but they are now openly and directly chosen by you and are not blindly accepted. New ones are added that fit your current situation, and the person you are.

Reflection: Think of a time when you felt guilty or ashamed, and then recall if the actions that produced the guilt or shame were not consistent with your values, or standards, or principles. Then think of a time when you did act in accord with these and recall how you felt at that time.

Try to accept reality without romanticizing it, without denying the negative or positive aspects. Try also to recognize how your perception might be distorted. The depressing aspects of reality are not ignored, neither are they emphasized to the extent that it seems futile to continue. Acceptance of reality is an adult response and can be a source of motivation to act to make the reality as constructive as possible.

Reflection: It isn't always pleasant to look at your reality, but when you can recognize the futility of arguing with verifiable facts or trying to get another person to change, you can begin to recognize fantasies, wishes, and dreams and recognize that these are unlikely to be realized. You will be better able to start to act in more constructive ways to benefit yourself and others, to make better decisions, and to see other alternatives and possibilities for solving problems.

Access your feelings and identify them. This is a major accomplishment, and one that contributes to a better understanding of oneself and of others. These emotions are neither shallow nor few in number. You are not fearful of knowing what you are feeling at all times, and this is a valuable source of information about what you are understanding and sensing. Your feelings are not always rational and logical, but that does not mean that they are not informative and valuable.

Reflection: Try and think of all of the feelings you have experienced today, up to this moment? How hard was that to do? Could you name all, just a few, or maybe none?

Perceptual Shift: Reduce Self-Absorption

It is relatively easy to see others' self-absorbed behaviors and attitudes, but it is not as easy to see your own. While it is reasonable to accept that you probably have some of these, it is also reasonable to try and work to reduce the self-absorbed behaviors and attitudes you may know you exhibit, as well as those that remain hidden to you.

Common Behaviors and Attitudes	Possible Self-Absorption
Taking on numerous tasks or responsibilities and feeling swamped.	Grandiosity
Exaggerating discomfort and aches and pains, or having multiple complaints.	Attention seeking
Dismissing or minimizing someone else's problem or concern as being trivial.	Lack of empathy
Having considerable self-doubt.	Impoverished ego

Lack of meaning and purpose in one's life.	Emptiness
Feeling that you are being treated unfairly and losing out while others don't have this happen to them.	Envy

These examples point out that self-absorbed behaviors and attitudes don't have to be intense, they can be milder versions of self-absorption. Reducing other similar behaviors and attitudes can be goals in your quest for your ideal self. Here are a few suggestions for how you may reduce these using the previous examples:

Reduce grandiosity. Stop when you start feeling swamped or overwhelmed with tasks, and reduce the number of tasks on your to-do list. Delegate some of those tasks (it's okay to ask for help sometimes), and accept that some tasks don't have to be done perfectly—good enough will be okay.

Reduce attention seeking. For example, don't deny that you have ailments or discomforts, but minimize these when talking to others unless they are able to provide you with relief. Start making it a habit to only talk about your ailments when assistance is needed.

Reduce lack of empathy. Even when a concern may be trivial, try to respond to that person's feelings about the concern or problem. You may not be able to be helpful with solutions for the concern, but you can recognize and respond to the person's feelings, which can be affirming and helpful.

Reduce impoverished ego. Whenever you encounter self-doubt or self-blame or feelings of inadequacy, you can use the positive self-statements you created to remind yourself that you do have competencies, abilities, and positive characteristics. You can even remind yourself that you are doing better with some things you are trying to improve.

Reduce emptiness. There are many paths to obtaining meaning and purpose in your life, such as connecting to others in meaningful ways, engaging in constructive works, finding inspiration, and appreciating your world. A couple of suggestions are to become a part of something positive and fulfilling, and to engage in altruistic acts. Reach out and connect to others authentically and with appreciation for their uniqueness.

Reduce or eliminate envy. It is relatively easy and common to be envious of others' achievements, successes, or talent. But that is a waste of your time and energy, which could be better spent on enhancing your strengths and learning new things. When I have an envious thought, I think about what I would have to give up to get what I am envious about or for.

Reflection: Think about the behaviors and attitudes described in this book as reflective of self-absorption, whether or not you feel that these describe you. For example, you may feel that the behavior "Exploitation of others" is not at all descriptive of you, but now think of what you or someone could do to reduce the particular behavior and attitude. Try this for all listed behaviors and attitudes. Then select two or three of the suggestions for changes you thought of that maybe you could implement even if you think you do not exhibit the behavior or attitude. For example, what could you do to reduce grandiosity even if you cannot see it in yourself.

Developing healthy adult narcissism is how you decrease your self-absorbed behaviors and attitudes and at the same time increase your self-reflection. Both are critical to prevent and reduce the amount of narcissistic wounding you may encounter. It may seem like a paradox to both focus on your self and to get out of your self, but a cohesive, centered, and grounded self requires that you become both less self-absorbed and more self-reflective.

Perceptual Shift: Increase Self-Reflection

Self-reflection is a way to examine what you are doing, feeling, and thinking to determine if you are unconsciously exhibiting self-absorbed behaviors and attitudes, whether your boundaries are appropriately strong and resilient, whether you are neglecting to take into account the needs of the other person, or whether you are in danger of becoming enmeshed or overwhelmed. Yes, you are focused on yourself, but in a different way than when that focus is self-absorbed. Examine the following to get an idea of what is meant by self-reflection.

Self-Absorbed	Self-Reflective
Am I doing it right?	I'm doing it okay, but can I improve.
I'm afraid of saying something wrong.	I want to respond appropriately and will try to tune in to what the other person is feeling.
I must be perfect.	I'll do my best, and accept that I may not be perfect.
I made a mistake and that's awful.	I can and will do better.
Everyone must like and approve of me or I am doomed to be rejected.	I want to be liked and to receive approval, but not at the expense of my integrity or values.

A necessary first step for increasing your self-reflection and decreasing self-absorption is to build your awareness of what you and others may be thinking and feeling in the moment. Suggested strategies for building your awareness include the following:

- Periodically and silently ask yourself to name, label, and identify what you are experiencing.

- Try to sense what other people may be feeling.

- Stay alert to your reactions as being projection or transference.

- Realize that your feelings may be misleading.

- Remind yourself of the limits of personal responsibility when interacting with others.

You are entitled to your feelings and no one else has a right to feel or suggest that you are wrong for having them. They are yours and should be respected. However, you can be misled by your feelings when you factor in your personality, your family-of-origin experiences, other past experiences, the extent of your self-absorption, and your emotional susceptibility. These are some major influences that determine what feelings are triggered for you. You may not consciously know that you are reacting to the present objective reality, but you are unconsciously reacting to these major factors. Staying aware of their possible influences can moderate your internal responses (some negative feelings may become less intense); help you make more constructive external responses; reduce any tendency you may have to personalize what others say and do; and help you learn to attend to others instead of always or mostly having your concern and attention on yourself.

Perceptual Shift: Develop Strong and Resilient Boundaries

Your psychological boundaries define where you are differentiated from others, and protect you from external assaults, such as others' projections that can lead to projective identifications. Developing strong and resilient boundaries will allow you to say no and stick to it, prevent you from being bullied or coerced into doing things that you don't want to do or that are not in your best interests, and help you resist attempts by others to mislead or con you. In addition, having strong and resilient boundaries is critical to all of the following relationship-enhancing thoughts, behaviors, and attitudes:

- Understand and respect the rights of others to have their differing opinions, perspectives, and so on, just as you have that right.

- Reduce or eliminate any conscious or unconscious tendency to exploit or manipulate others by accepting that others do not exist to serve you. Make a habit of doing as much for yourself as possible, not asking others to do what you could do for yourself, and being as independent as possible while preserving your relationships.

- Do not expect others to have the same values, standards, or beliefs as you do, and recognize that they are separate, unique, and worthwhile individuals. Accept and recognize that others' values and standards may also have some validity.

- Reduce or eliminate your emotional susceptibility so that you do not become enmeshed or over whelmed by others' projections or emotions. Work to become more confident that what you are thinking and feeling is not contaminated by others' emotional sending that you are unconsciously catching.

- Become better able to repel external assaults, such as projections, and avoid incorporating them into your essential inner self and acting on them. Although much of this usually happens on an unconscious level, your increased awareness of your emotional susceptibility and taking a few steps to moderate this will allow you to act in your best interests and on your values.

- Protect your essential inner self while at the same time having respect for others' inner essential selves.

These are very important outcomes, and sufficient boundary strength can do the most important thing of all, that is, prevent you from narcissistic wounding. With sufficient boundary strength, others' cutting, criticizing, and blaming comments do not get to your essential inner self and inflict wounds; you are less likely to have your guilt and shame triggered; you rely more on your self-perception and self-values that were examined and freely chosen for your guidance and direction, and you do not take responsibility for others' thoughts and feelings.

It takes time and effort to build your boundary strength and it will not happen overnight. So be patient with yourself and resolve to stick with your program. The program begins with a self-assessment to try to pinpoint when and how your boundaries are breached. For example, are there particular people, times, or events that seem to easily overwhelm you with emotions, demands, or expectations and you end up doing things you don't want to do? Could it be that you are so open to others that you become easily enmeshed and act more in accord with the other person's feelings than on your own feelings? This self-reflection can be valuable to help you determine the steps you can take.

The next step could be to reduce your emotional susceptibility, so that you don't have to have rigid boundaries where no one can get to you, or soft boundaries where almost everyone can get to you, or spongy boundaries where others can unexpectedly get to you. You can reduce this susceptibility in a number of ways, and you must find what works for you. In the short term, these are some nonverbal strategies that can help:

- Orient your body away from the other person. Stand or sit so that you are somewhat turned away from that person.

- Look at the person's forehead, just past the person's ears, or even across the room. Don't maintain eye contact.

- Bring another person into the conversation. Look around and call someone to join you.

- Change the topic when you sense that your emotions are intensifying, or that the other person is trying to manipulate you.

- Keep a barrier of some sort between you and the other person. Anything can serve as a barrier; toss pillows, a purse, a book, or any medium-sized object.

- Leave, move away, or take a break (for example, bathroom) when you begin to feel the slightest discomfort.

Other behaviors such as these can do much to reduce the incidences where your emotional susceptibility lead you to be overwhelmed or enmeshed.

Once you can do some of these things to reduce your emotional susceptibility, you can begin to also concentrate on strengthening your understanding of your self as separate and distinct from others. That's where the true boundary strength is, and your nonconscious and unconscious understanding of this is where the real work is done. This makes if difficult, but it is not impossible as people can and do grow and develop throughout their lives.

Perceptual Shifts: Cultivate Your Strengths

Many people have unrecognized or unused strengths, and you may be one of them. You may emphasize your faults and flaws more than you celebrate your strengths. After all, these perceived shortcomings are your shame, and you work to overcome having to feel this most uncomfortable feeling. What I want to suggest is that you begin to make a shift to emphasizing and cultivating your strengths. That shift would not mean that you would ignore your shortcomings and flaws. No, you would continue to work on these, but you would take a fresh look at your strengths so that you can better capitalize on those. It is much easier to build on strengths than it is to remediate weaknesses or deficits. This process will also lead you to greater and more realistic self-acceptance and help to fortify you against external assaults, such as demeaning and devaluing remarks.

What are your strengths? You probably have some strengths you are overlooking, and are not aware of others. If you are like many people, you think of your strengths in terms of what others have noticed or complimented you for. That can be limiting because you cannot always count on others to comment on or compliment your strengths. Further, you may have some flaws or weaknesses that you don't realize are concealing strengths. For example, some people may think that focusing on details is a weakness. It can be when carried to excess, but embedded in that behavior and attitude is a strength, because such focusing reduces or eliminates mistakes. Indeed, in some professions and jobs it is essential that the primary focus be on details, for example, preparing a room for surgery, food presentation, events planning, or proofreading.

Some more examples may be helpful:

Flaw or Weakness	Possible Embedded Strength
Makes blunt direct comments	Genuine, leaves little doubt as to what is meant.
Stubborn	Has the courage of their convictions, maintains personal value system, is decisive.
Dreamy	Imaginative, visualizes possibilities.
Indecisive	Alert to many possible options and alternatives.

You now have list of strengths to cultivate. As you focus on and cultivate these strengths, you can reduce, moderate, or eliminate the flaws or weaknesses. Let's go back to the example of attention to details to get some notion of how this can work. The strength could be a reduction of possible errors or mistakes. Therefore, the person could work to reduce these, but also set a personal limit for how much checking and attention is good enough or acceptable. The person could start to accept that others do not have this characteristic and realize that it is not reasonable to demand that others also have this attention to details. In other words, accept it about yourself, but don't expect others to have it. Then, too, you would want to take care that the need to attend to details doesn't become excessive.

Perceptual Shift: Become Your Own Person

You may be asking what does it mean to become your own person and how does one do that? Becoming your own person means that you are separated and individuated so that you are clear where you end and where others begin. This may sound a bit abstract, but it is what is psychologically and developmentally expected for adults. That is, psychologically mature adults perceive themselves as able to do all of the following:

- They choose their values, principles, and standards after careful consideration of these, instead of blindly accepting what others tell them.

- They are respectful of themselves and of others.

- They act in accordance with their personal ethics and morals and are not unduly influenced to ignore or reject these to please others.

- They recognize that others are unique and special as individuals and are entitled to respect and tolerance.

- They connect to others in meaningful and satisfying ways.

- They recognize and reject toxic relationships.

- They can resist being controlled or manipulated by others.

- They are creative and ever growing and changing.

Let's examine each of these indices of being your own person with healthy adult narcissism.

Examine your values, principles, and standards, and choose those that you feel best fit you as you are today. This examination can also help you determine if you are continuing to act on values you unconsciously incorporated, or on values that were taught or imposed on you but that are not a part of who you want to be. You can now make a conscious effort to discard things that no longer work for you, that are at odds with the person you think you are or the person you want to become, and you can select new values that you have examined and freely chosen.

During this examination period, you can also reflect on your actions and measure these against your values. Failure to live up to your values can produce guilt, and acting in accord with your values is one way to reduce or eliminate some guilt feelings.

Act in accord with your personal ethics and morals. Doing this will keep you on the right track and permit you to reduce occasions of feeling shamed. In addition, you can ensure that you are not unduly influenced by others to reject or ignore these just to please someone else. Your actions speak louder than your words, and you want your actions to be consistent with what you believe.

You may want to take some time to reflect on just what ethical principles and moral beliefs you have. Ethics are the principles of right and wrong, and morals are the goodness or badness of actions and character. The following exercise may assist in clarifying your ethics and morals.

Respect yourself and respect others. This sounds so simple, but in reality it is very complex. Respect includes an awareness of self and others as being separate, distinct, unique, and worthy. Physical and psychological boundaries are recognized, and actions convey this recognition and acceptance. It could be helpful to remember that those with a DNP, and others who have some aspects of undeveloped narcissism, cannot recognize and accept their boundaries and those of others. They violate these because they fail to recognize them, think that they are entitled to do so, dismiss them as unimportant, do not care, or have failed to develop a sense of where they end and where others begin. Respecting yourself means:

- Refusing to be manipulated into doing things you do not want to do, or which are not in your best interests, just to be accommodating or to please another person.

- When you say no, you mean it and are not bullied or coerced into changing your mind.

- Acting in accord with your carefully considered ethics, morals, values, standards, and principles.

Indications of respect for others include civility and courtesy in interactions, acceptance of differences in opinion and values, and recognizing others' positive characteristics. One word of caution, don't expect that you or anyone else are entitled to get their way just because they express their opinion, and the other person listens and accepts it. Listening and accepting is respect, and that is all anyone should expect.

Connect to others in meaningful ways and you will enrich your life. This refers to all your relationships, family, friends, other social relationships, work, and so on. Some of the elements of a meaningful relationship are as follows:

- Mutual respect and acceptance

- Respect for each other's psychological boundaries

- Empathy

- Trust

- Openness and directness when expressing emotions, wants, needs, and desires

- Sensitivity to each other's moods, needs, and so on

- Giving and receiving support and encouragement

- Concern for the other person's welfare and well-being

- Dependability and responsibility

Relationships provide a feeling of personal attachment, of social integration, of being nurtured, and of reassurance that you are valued and worthy. Your meaningful relationships reduce or eliminate loneliness and isolation, help you cope with stress, protect your health, and are related to resilience, hardiness, and optimism. The positives are many and strong.

Reject toxic relationships. It can be easy to become involved in a relationship that becomes dissatisfying, and some of these relationships can even be toxic. What usually happens is that the relationship becomes toxic over time, or the other person is able to hide their toxicity. Either way, you may not recognize the negative effects the relationship is having on you. You may care for the person and want to preserve the relationship, so you then try harder and harder to please that person so that they will like or love you, be appreciative and approve of you, and other things that comprise a positive relationship. What you are likely to find is that you have to give up or compromise important pieces of your inner essential self in order to keep that relationship, and that is what makes a relationship toxic. It is important that you be able to recognize when a relationship is toxic and negative and be able to reject it and focus on initiating, forming, and maintaining meaningful and enduring relationships that are enriching for your life.

Others. The other people you encounter and relate to impact and influence you. It can be helpful to the relationship to carefully consider others' desires and needs, and to not be mostly or entirely focused on your own desires and needs. However, you also do not want to give others' desires and needs so much importance that yours are ignored or neglected, or attend to them to the extent that you become controlled, manipulated, or confined. There is a balance that must be found and maintained.

Central to finding and maintaining this balance is identifying and relinquishing your faulty beliefs about what you are to be and to do. Some faulty beliefs that may be affecting you are the following:

- I should be perfect and berate myself when I fall short.

- I should never make mistakes because mistakes are shameful.

- I am responsible for how others feel and I have to stay alert to ensure that they only have positive feelings.

- Others must treat me fairly, and it's my fault when they do not.

- It's my fault if I am rejected, it means I am fatally flawed.

- I'm to blame if things don't go my way, or as I planned them, because I'm not adequate enough.

- If I love someone, that person must love me in return or I will be destroyed.

- Everyone must like and approve of me in order for me to feel adequate.

Creative, ever growing, and ever changing. Do not allow yourself to be static, complacent, and stuck in your ways, refusing to change and grow. You are never too old to learn something new, to continue to be creative in many ways, or to grow and change. It's not so much that you are searching for something, but rather that you are enhancing the self that you have developed and love.

Build your creativity by looking at your world with the intent of seeing something that you did not see before, and of seeking new ways of expressing yourself through your works and everyday life. Trying new processes, developing new and novel things, and even thinking in new ways are all parts of creativity. If you are so inclined, you may want to sample the creative and performing arts, to experience what they are like and what they release or develop within you. You have to seek these out, they don't look for you. But what you may find is that you are enriched and enhanced with participation.

Self-building strategies. There are numerous ways to engage in enriching and building your essential inner self. Some specific suggestions include the following:

- Don't expect others to fix you, rescue you, or make you happy. Learn to be in charge of your own happiness, ask for help only when needed, and accept that you may need some changing but basically you are okay.

- Cultivate hope, optimism, and altruism, as these are states that promote a sense of well-being.

- Don't obsess about that which you cannot control or change. Work to change the things that you can change and let go of control over uncontrollable events and situations.

- Plan to frequently learn something new, try novel approaches to usual tasks, and embrace your creativity.

- Be patient and accepting of yourself. Think of setbacks as learning opportunities and resolve to do better next time.

- Visualize the person you want to be and work to become that person.

To become your own person requires considerable self-examination and choosing your beliefs, attitudes, and values. You examine those you currently possess, judge their usefulness for your life, and think about how these define you as a person. This examination allows you to reject some qualities you have incorporated and acted on without conscious thought, to keep those you think fit you, and to develop others you want to have but did not consciously understand that you did not have.

You can behave in ways that show respect for the uniqueness and value of yourself, and you can also extend this respect and acceptance to others. You can become accepting and comfortable with individual differences, but also allow yourself to be as you are without demanding that everyone be like you or that you must be like others. Differences in others are not perceived as threats to who you are.

Other positive outcomes for becoming your own person can include the following:

- You become less dependent on others' approval and lessen your need for external validation, so that when you do not get these you are not disappointed.

- You can control and manage your anxiety better so that you do not act in ways that tend to intensify the anxiety, or that can cause you to act contrary to your values and ethics.

- You can value the input of others and listen and reflect on what they tell you, but you act in accord with your inner essential self.

- You use your deeper understanding of yourself and of others to become more creative, to promote the viability of your relationships, and to be centered and grounded.

Given all these positives, becoming your own person is a worthwhile endeavor. Some of the work you can do yourself through self-reflection and self-exploration, some of the work can be done when completing the exercises in this book, and some may need the guidance and expertise of a mental health professional. The latter can be especially helpful when exploring family-of-origin factors. You will be pleased at what happens for you when you put forth the effort to become your own person, and give up beliefs, perceptions, attitudes, and values that you unquestionably accepted and acted in accord with but that did not fit with who you wanted to be. You are now determining the person you want to be and acting to make it happen. The modest changes proposed in this chapter are a start; they are doable and you can begin to formulate your own set of shifts.

CHAPTER ACTIVITIES

Identify Your Strengths

Materials: A sheet of paper, a writing instrument, eight or ten 3 by 1 strips of different colored paper, and a glue stick.

Procedure:

1. Take the strips of paper and write one strength of yours on each strip.

2. Use the glue stick to glue each strip down on one side of the paper.

3. Review what you wrote on the strips you pasted.

4. Now, write a summary about your strengths.

Suggestions for possible strengths:

- I am resilient—able to bounce back from adversity.

- I have a fighting spirit—I do not give up in the face of opposition.

- I am organized and can plan complex projects—work, family dinners, and so on.

- I am neat—I keep things in their proper places where they can be found when needed.

- I do not panic in a crisis.

- I am sensitive to others' feelings and concerns.

- I am energetic and outgoing.

Visualization

Recall a grudge or resentment you may have relative to your self-absorbed parent. Close your eyes, visualize the grudge or resentment, and allow it to float away on a leaf blowing in the wind, or floating down a creek.

CHAPTER 9

Get to the Ideal:
Build a New and Better Self

Introduction

Let's take a look at the person you want to be so that you have an opportunity to determine if your ideal self that you want to become is realistic and achievable, or if you have unrealistic and unobtainable goals. You will want to have goals that have a good probability of attainment so that you increase your satisfaction with your essential inner self, thereby increasing your self-esteem, self-confidence, and self-efficacy. Examining your current self versus your ideal self can also identify where you need to make changes and where you have made changes that bring you closer to your desired goal, and suggest some specific strategies that may be helpful.

Before moving further, let's recap some of what has been presented to this point. Chapter 7 presented some strategies to strengthen your essential inner self that included how to build meaning and purpose for your life that reflect your choices, values, and principles; techniques and strategies to reduce or eliminate feelings of isolation and alienation, and some of the self-absorbed behaviors and attitudes that may be negatively affecting your relationships; and how to become more centered and grounded, so that your choices and decisions are not unduly influenced by what others, such as your self-absorbed parent, think you should be and do.

Chapter 8 focused on giving more information on strengthening your essential inner self by increasing your awareness in the moment, revealing how self-reflection is helpful, identifying and using your strengths, the value of strong and resilient psychological boundaries, and acting in accord with your ethics, values, principles, and morals. The emphasis was on how you can be more fully alive.

This chapter continues to provide suggestions for how to develop and strengthen your essential inner self, how to act as an adult with your self-absorbed parent, and how to develop and maintain meaningful relationships. Addressed in this chapter are how your early experiences may have impacted you and may be continuing to do so, the value of sympathic and reflective responding to your self-absorbed parent and others, steps to take to become stronger and more resilient, and improving your relationships.

The Role of Early Experiences in Shaping You

Your inner essential self develops over time, and its growth is influenced by an interaction of the care and nurturing and other experiences you received during your formative years from your family of origin, your past experiences with people other than your family of origin, and personality characteristics that are innately yours. Each person's inner essential self is different, and people may differ in subtle ways even if they have similar environmental influences.

There is a considerable body of knowledge about the psychological growth and development of the self, and in every case, researchers and theorists emphasize that the quality of early care and nurturing received is a critical component. "Early," in this case, means the period from birth through the earliest formative years. There are some studies on prenatal influences, but these have not been tied to the psychological development of the self and are more focused on physical influences that can play a role in psychological development. We will not explore this information, as it is not directly tied to psychological development.

The basic question is, "How did you come to be as you are today?" What is presented here is some information to guide your self-exploration of your psychological development, which in turn may provide some clues as to why you may continue to be narcissistically wounded, help you to get a better perspective, and show you ways to ward off some wounding experiences. Your perception of your self is an important part of this, and your understanding of some possible early influences and experiences can be of immense help.

Let's begin with a reflection about some early messages you received about how you were perceived by your parents and siblings.

Reflection: Try and recall the thoughts and feelings you had about yourself as a child, especially those that were the products of what you were told about how your parent(s) or siblings perceived your intelligence and your physical appearance, how pleasing or not you were to them just for being and not for what you did for them, and whether or not they smiled or complimented you. How might you have internalized these experiences and continued to feel about yourself and act on those today? Are these still valid for the person you are today?

You may find that you are presenting yourself and reacting to others from the early messages you received from others about your physical appearance or intelligence or abilities or other qualities rather than reacting from your current reality or experiencing.

These early messages have become so incorporated into your essential inner self that you may not even be aware of their existence until you take the time to reflect on them. They are an ingrained part of who you are, but you unconsciously incorporated them and identified with them without conscious intent as you were a child at that time. These unconscious early messages continue to affect your self-perception today and can play a role in determining the extent to which you become narcissistically wounded, especially in interactions with your self-absorbed parent. The next section describes how you can better manage interactions with the parent with the use of sympathetic reflective listening and responding.

Sympathetic and Reflective Responding to Your Self-Absorbed Parent .

This section describes how to better manage interactions with your self-absorbed parent. It can also be helpful for other interactions and relationships. You can be more effective if you learn to use reflective listening and responding. It is not helpful for you to try to be empathic with the self-absorbed parent, but that does not mean that you cannot notice the feelings directly or indirectly expressed in the parent's communications and interactions. The first thing is to distinguish between empathy and a more helpful way for you to identify and respond to your parent's feelings. Doing so will enable the parent to feel heard and understood without you having to agree or buy in to the parent's message or feelings.

Do you confuse empathy and sympathy? You can respond to or sympathize with your self-absorbed parent without opening yourself up to potentially catching the parent's projections or feelings and then making these your own and acting on them. You don't have to always either become enmeshed or overwhelmed by someone else's feelings or shut the other person out completely. It can be helpful for you to be able to use reflective responding with your self-absorbed parent and with others. Reflective responding does not demand that you feel what the other person feels, which you would do in empathic responding. Reflective responding has four steps:

1. Identify the feeling the other person has (whether that person expresses that feeling directly or indirectly).

2. Verbalize (reflect) the feeling without repeating exactly what the other person said or what you think that person meant. Do not add anything to the reflection, such as a question. Example: "You seem irritated."

3. Wait for confirmation or disconfirmation of your identification of the feeling before adding your input or asking a question. The other person will correct you if you are wrong or if that person doesn't like your word choice. For example, if you reflected their anger, their response to that may be to correct you by saying that they are not angry but that they are annoyed. At that point you can stop talking and wait for the person to elaborate or explain. Accept any correction of the feeling the person makes.

4. At that point you can ask a question or make your input. Try to not argue with the self-absorbed parent or to present another viewpoint. The goal is to recognize the other person's feelings.

Another task when you are beginning to make reflective responses is to practice identifying the feeling expressed by another person who is not expressing the feeling directly but expressing a thought about a feeling. For example, what could be the feeling of the speaker in the following statements?

"You're wonderful!"

"I'm uncomfortable."

"It's a beautiful day."

"I don't like this."

"Why are you doing that?"

If you know the speaker well, you may be able to accurately guess what that person is feeling. On the other hand, even if you do think you know the person, you are just as likely to be wrong in your guess as to be right. The person may think they are speaking directly and accurately, but their feelings are concealed and indirect. Further, there could be several possible feelings for each statement. So it is not easy to identify the feelings. For the sake of discussion, let's suppose that the following feelings in italics are the ones the person is experiencing:

"You're wonderful." (I'm very *pleased* with what you did.)

"I'm uncomfortable." (I'm *jittery* or *apprehensive* about what may be coming next.)

"It's a beautiful day." (I'm *happy* and glad to be alive.)

"I don't like this." (I'm *fearful* about the outcome.)

"Why are you doing that?" (What you are doing is very *irritating.*)

The next steps would be for you to respond by speaking the feeling (reflection) first, and then adding what you want to say. For example, the exchange for the first two statements may go like this:

"You're wonderful!"

Response: "You are pleased with what I did, and I appreciate that I was able to please you."

"I'm uncomfortable."

Response: "You seem anxious and jittery. What seems to be causing this reaction?"

Notice that you first respond by letting the person know that you understand what the person may be feeling before you give your input. All this seems pretty simple and easy, but it can be difficult to change if reflecting is not how you customarily respond.

Reflection: For one day, pay attention to how often you respond without first reflecting the direct or indirect feelings back to the speaker. The next day practice reflecting feelings first and note how your conversations flow. This is especially effective with children.

Practice identifying feelings and giving a reflecting response, and you will find that you will also get better at making empathic responses. When you feel that your boundaries are sufficiently strong and resilient, you can begin to open yourself so that you really feel what the other person is feeling without losing yourself in that person's emotions, or losing the sense of yourself as separate and distinct from that person. That is, you can be empathic. Until you can reach this point, you will be better served in interactions with your self-absorbed parent to limit your responses to a more distant reflective one.

Before ending this section, let's give some more examples of reflective responses to your self-absorbed parent who says things designed to demean, devalue, or upset you. You don't have to take offense, to let this get to you, to fight back, to agree with the put-downs, or even to be reflective. Then, why even bother giving a reflective response? Because such a response can help keep the focus on the parent or other person, and that protects you from catching that person's feelings or projections, acknowledges that person's feelings and intent, but does not commit you to agreeing or disagreeing.

Self-Absorbed Parent: "You don't ever seem to be able to get it right."

Reflective Response: "You're unhappy with what I did (or said)." Or: "It bothers you when things are not done right."

Self-Absorbed Parent:	"Brian is so much more intelligent (handsome, talented, or the like) than you are."
Reflective Response:	"You really admire Brian."
Self-Absorbed Parent:	"You look silly (doing, wearing) that."
Reflective Response:	"You dislike what I'm (doing, wearing)."
Self-Absorbed Parent:	"Why on earth would you do something dumb like that?"
Reflective Response:	"You're annoyed that I did not live up to your expectations for me."

These are only examples of some of the many different kinds of reflective responses you could make. What you can find out when you use responses such as these is that it gives you time to think instead of immediately triggering your negative feelings, it puts the focus on the other person and that person's feelings, and allows that person to clarify what they meant, in case you were in error when you identified the feeling.

Becoming Stronger Through Creative Endeavors

Creativity appears in many forms. Your first task is to become more open and aware of your potential for creativity, your creative endeavors, and the wide range of possibilities that are available for you to explore that will enhance and expand your creativity. Creativity is not always associated with artistic talent, and it will be helpful for you to not limit yourself with this thought. If you are linking the two, then you may think that only some people can be creative, or that you can be creative in only one or two ways, or that you must have an inborn ability or capacity. Yes, when you look at people who receive recognition of their talents and creativity, they do seem to fit the last description. However, the definition and description we will use here are the hallmarks of healthy adult narcissism, available to everyone. They can be developed and are not dependent on innate talent.

Creativity, as used here, includes developing new ways to do things and solve problems by trying new perspectives, engaging in creating something that brings you pleasure (a product, a process, or a thought), learning something you did not know and making constructive use of that new knowledge, streamlining, correcting, reducing, or eliminating barriers, constraints, and roadblocks; and attempting something different. There is a popular saying about thinking outside the box. Thinking outside of usual confinements and assumptions means thinking in new and different ways, thinking from other perspectives and being open to trying what has not been tried before. The first step is being willing to reach out for new ideas, thoughts, and so on.

Engaging in creative endeavors can do all of the following for you:

- Promote feelings of joy and satisfaction that extends to many facets of your life.

- Find it easier to screen out distractions, worries, and other concerns for periods of time.

- Help with healing wounds to the essential inner self.

- Access overlooked or unrealized aspects of your self that can be enriching.

However, not all benefits are personal for you. When you think creatively you can extend your new perspectives to showing care and concern for your family, such as creating new meals; you can beautify your environment, either inside (home) or outside (yard); you can save money by fixing the stuff that breaks or doesn't function well; you can bring beauty into your life and that of others; you can demonstrate problem-solving that teaches others how to better solve their problems; and you can encourage and support others' creativity. You can model excitement and curiosity, which can be catching. You are teaching by example how to be open and how to be accepting of challenges.

When you are creative, you are not locked inside yourself; you are more available to others and have a zest and excitement in your life. These are all very positive outcomes for developing your creativity.

Each person will have an individual way to unleash their creativity; your challenge will be to find your own unique one. You'll have to try a lot of things before you find those that suit you, but don't become discouraged. Keep trying and you'll find it. To get started, you can do one or more of the following:

- Recall what you did that gave you pleasure as a child that could be a creative endeavor today, and do it.

- Take a class in something that interests you.

- Buy a kit from a craft store and complete it.

- Pull out your cookbook, look in a magazine, or go online and try some new recipes.

- Sketch your surroundings.

- Write anything—a poem, or a story, or an essay, or just write.

- Find a new use for something you intend to throw away.

You are best person to decide what would be creative for you. Just go ahead and do it.

Connecting to Inspiration

Spirituality or inspiration has been found to be of physical, emotional, and psychological benefit. It encompasses religion, but is more extensive than religion. In fact, you don't have to be religious when you are also spiritual. Since there are many who will reject the notion of spirituality, fearing that you mean religion, I've elected to term the concept "inspirational." This will be defined as the space between existing and acting where you transcend yourself and become connected to the universe. Inspirational is the uplifting, encouraging, sustaining, and joyous realm where you can feel less isolated and alienated, even when alone, because of the deep connectedness to the universe you feel to be a part of your life.

Becoming inspired or looking for inspiration can help you build stronger connections to yourself, to others, and to the universe. It can also reduce feelings of being isolated and lonely, becoming alienated, or just feeling adrift without direction. Inspiration can assist you to find centeredness and to become more grounded and balanced.

Why cultivate inspiration? How can this make a difference in giving up grudges, resentments, and so on? How does inspiration do anything to prevent or moderate narcissistic wounding? Inspiration works in indirect ways, as do so many other aspects of your life. It helps you be optimistic, hopeful, resilient, less prone to beating up on your essential inner self, and better able to accept yourself as you are and others as they are. You become better able to not sweat the small stuff, to recognize what is relevant and what is not, and you stay focused on the important things for your life.

Earlier in the book we identified feelings of helplessness and hopelessness as part of the narcissistic wounding. The guilt and shame that can be aroused is a part of what keeps the wounds from healing. Sometimes, no amount of external support and approval, positive self-talk, or even success is sufficient to mitigate these negative effects on the self. We have all read about extremely successful people who are admired and get positive attention but who continue to do self-destructive things, or who write that they do not believe they are good enough. Such cases illustrate how devastating and persistent the narcissistic wounding can be.

You've probably made some progress on healing your wounds and in developing and fortifying your essential inner self to prevent, eliminate, or reduce this wounding. Keep working and you will get better. Adding inspiration is another positive step that will pay dividends with positive outcomes.

There are many ways to get in touch with your inspirational life and to help grow and expand it. Sometimes you can even access it through other parts of your life, such as the creative process, your work, or your service to others. However you get to it, you will find that it lifts and enhances your spirit, helps with meaning and purpose, inoculates and sustains you during adversity, and increases your awareness and enjoyment of your life.

Other ways to get in touch with your inspirational life include the following. Select those that best fit you, try one or more that are new to you, and pay attention to what emerges for you. None will work immediately, but any can work over time.

- Meditation

- Religion and prayer

- Creative endeavors

- Reading inspirational books

- Writing your expressive thoughts

- Centering and grounding ceremonies

- Relationship cultivation and strengthening

Mutual Respect and Acceptance

Respect for each other as unique, worthwhile, and valued individuals is basic for a strong and loving relationship. You want to feel cherished, you want to feel that you matter, that you are significant and important in the other person's life, and you give the same in return. Acceptance, like respect, is focused on other people as they are, not as you want them to be, or only if they change. Acceptance as you are does not mean you cannot or should not change some behaviors. For example, if neatness is important to the other person and you tend to not be neat, you may want to try to be neater as long as the demand for neatness is not excessive.

Gain Empathic Attunement for Your Important Relationships

Empathy is a wonderful experience where the person feels fully understood. It is also a rare experience. Some people equate empathy with sympathy, or in becoming overwhelmed or enmeshed in someone's feelings, but these states are not what is meant by empathy. These are cognitive responses in the case of sympathy, and lack of boundary strength for the other two. Empathy occurs when you can sense the inner experiencing of the other person and tune in to what is being felt *without* losing your sense of yourself as being separate and distinct from the other person. You are not left with residual feelings that you are unable to let go of, which is what happens when you become overwhelmed or enmeshed.

Empathy is also important for meaningful and satisfying relationships, and in relationships empathy should also be reciprocal. You must both give and receive empathy, and not have this as one-sided in the relationship. It is not necessary to always be empathic, but it is important to be frequently empathic.

Do not confuse empathy with agreement with your feeling, or with sympathy. Just because someone understands what you are feeling does not mean that that person agrees with your feeling or with your rationale. For example, suppose you are angry and hurt at a remark made by a friend. Your partner can empathize with your anger and hurt, but can still retain enough separation and individuation to not agree that your friend's remark was insensitive, even though it appeared that way to you. Countless fights and disagreements have resulted from an expectation that empathy meant agreement, when one person became angry because she felt that if her partner really loved her and understood how she felt, then he would agree with her.

A Balance of Fun and Responsibility

An element of fun and playfulness enlivens any meaningful relationship. But unless that element is counterbalanced with responsibility on the part of both parties in an intimate relationship, then one party has to assume all or most of the responsibility. This situation can lead to developing negative feelings, where one person is focused on play and fun, and the other person keeps trying to get him to recognize and accept his responsibilities.

Fun and play bring out some childlike qualities, which can be endearing and can arouse one's delight and wonder. Both of you want the other to enjoy and participate in each other's version of fun and play.

Adult responsibilities are many, and there are times when they can appear to be overwhelming and you wish you had fewer of them, or that you could get away for a while. However, you probably just keep on trying to meet your responsibilities even if you complain about them. Think about your current lover or spouse. Does that person meet their responsibilities most of the time? Or is that person mostly focused on pleasure, fun, play, and the like? If the latter is the case, then fun and play are not counterbalanced with responsibility.

Well-Placed Trust

Some people end up in more than one unsuitable relationship because they inappropriately trust others. Regardless of negative experiences such as betrayal, they rush back to bestowing their trust in someone rather than reflecting on their deep need to trust, and working through their feelings of betrayal.

Trust is a bedrock for meaningful, satisfying, and enduring relationships. Trust produces the following feelings and assumptions about the other person in the relationship:

- The other person cares for you and has concern for your welfare.

- The other person is usually open and truthful in interactions with you.

- The other person understands, values, and cherishes you and the relationship.

- The other person wants the same type of relationship that you do, including the level of commitment.

- The other person will not mislead you or push you to do things you do not want to do just for that person's needs or benefit.

Does this describe how you usually perceive the other person in your relationships? You may want to take some time to reflect on your past relationships and recall some of your feelings, attitudes, motives, and so on, about the other person to see of you acted in accord with the above description, that is, you had considerable trust in the other person. If you have failed relationships that involved betrayal of trust, then you may want to reflect on what you are seeking that allows you to overlook or ignore signs of betrayal or lack of trustworthiness. Yes, the other person acted badly, but you wanted the relationship so much that you did not take care of yourself, and it could be helpful to better understand your motives.

Openness of Emotional Expression

Trying to guess what someone is feeling can be very frustrating, even when you know the person very well, as there are occasions when what is felt or experienced is hidden or masked. Strong relationships are usually those where both partners are willing to be open in their emotional expressions and are aware of the impact of those expressions on the other person. Both are important for the relationship, because the other person may not be in a state or place where they can hear and understand your feelings, or vice versa.

There are some people who do have difficulty openly expressing their feelings because of early family-of-origin experiences where open expression was not encouraged, or was actively discouraged. In addition, some people have had experiences where they were ignored or hurt when they did express their feelings. Still others are unaware of experiencing mild versions of feelings, such as annoyance, and can only express very intense ones, usually in an inappropriate way. One or more of these descriptions may fit you or your partner.

Relinquish Resentments and Grudges

An important part of building a new and better self is to let go of negative things that are sapping your energy, time, and creativity, and that are not constructive. Resentments and grudges fall into this category, and letting go is a part of the building process. Think of it as building being constructive, and resentments and grudges as destructive. Sometimes you have to destroy something in the process of building new structures. You are encouraged to build a new you, one that is your ideal self, and in order to build the constructive and positive parts of your inner essential self, you may need to destroy some of the negative structures.

You may have started reading this book with lots of resentment and grudges against your self-absorbed parent for the early and persistent narcissistic wounding you experienced. Although you may now better understand how the parent wounded you in unconscious and subtle ways that continue to affect your self-esteem and your relationships, that does not mean that you are ready to forgive and forget, nor is forgiving and forgetting being pushed here.

Forgiveness

I'm often asked if the child of a self-absorbed parent should or has to forgive that parent, and my answer is no. Forgiveness may be possible at some point, but it is not a requirement. The child was injured at a deep level, is still being negatively impacted as an adult, and the child's energies are better spent on more positive pursuits, such as developing their own undeveloped narcissism and establishing meaningful relationships.

The sense of relief is palpable and visible after receiving my answer, and people tell me how awful they were feeling because they could not forgive. I usually respond that they may want to forgive at some future time when they have completed enough personal work and reflection where forgiveness seems possible. It's much easier to encourage forgiveness if you are an outsider, and did not have to experience the daily or constant assaults on the self by the self-absorbed parent, who in many cases is continuing these assaults. The self of the adult child has to be fortified and developed to withstand these assaults, to further grow and prosper in positive ways, and to receive internal and external validation of their meaning and worth in order to be in a place where forgiveness is possible. Don't forget that the parent probably felt and thought all of the following, and continues to do so even though you are now an adult:

- I was right to do what I did.

- I was entitled to do what I did.

- The child is wrong and shameful to question my actions, needs, and demands.

- If my child was worthy, they would be appreciative of me.

- I should be admired.

- If it were not for me, my child would be a mess.

- I know better what my child needs than she does.

- My child is too sensitive and overreacts to my constructive (in reality they are destructive) comments.

- Whatever I did was for her own good, and I was the best judge of that.

- That child owes me everything.

It is an extremely rare person who can experience these self-absorbed parental attitudes without reexperiencing some of the negative feelings that may have been present since childhood. It is also challenging and rare to be able to withstand these, and to see beyond them to perceive that the parent is experiencing bleakness, fear, and isolation. The parent could have so much that is worthwhile, but has nothing and doesn't know how to enrich their life. Enrichment of your life has to come from within, and the self-absorbed parent has few if any inner resources.

The deep emotional ties between parent and child can prevent the adult child from being objective and completely logical about a self-absorbed parent, so that parent's negative actions, comments, and responses can continue to hurt. This too makes forgiveness difficult, if not impossible.

It may be more helpful for you as an adult to not worry about forgiveness, but to keep that in mind as a possible option when the time is right; to not try to force yourself to forgive because others think it is the right thing to do, and to focus more on some interim steps that help your healing. Let's try to identify some indications of healing that can be suggestive of interim steps.

- You can reflect on your parent and accept that the parent is unlikely to change, and that you don't strongly yearn or wish that the parent would change. While change is possible, you accept that you cannot force, mandate, demand, or influence the parent to change.

- Your parent's negative, demeaning, and devaluing comments don't hurt as much, and their negative impact is not as long lasting. These comments can still wound, but that wounding is becoming less.

- You may still dread interactions with your self-absorbed parent, but you don't leave these interactions as churned up as you did before; their effects don't last as long and you are able to be more detached during them. You are also containing and managing your feelings better.

- You are more aware of the possibility that your reactions to your parent can get displaced onto others, and you consciously work to not let this happen.

- You are better able to be empathic, and this has improved your most important relationships.

- You are more centered and grounded, and do not respond to the parent either in a compliant way or by being defiant. You also are more aware of when you may be reacting or relating to others as you did with your parent.

- At some level, you realize that you have the power to prevent your parent from hurting you so much, and that you can choose to have a more measured, less hurtful response to the self-absorbed parent that does not disrespect either of you .

- You derive satisfaction from your other relationships and give these your time, effort, and energies, and receive much in return.

- You are able to reach out to others in your most intimate relationships, to sense their feelings without becoming enmeshed or overwhelmed or wanting to get away; and you are able to connect with others in a deep and meaningful way.

When your essential inner self feels ready to forgive, that is the time and you can proceed. You may never fully reach this point, and that is understandable, not shameful There is no need to feel guilty for not being able to forgive. You need time to heal before you can forgive.

We are now at the end of this journey, but you are only beginning your journey to heal your essential inner self, to fortify yourself against narcissistic injury, and to let go of the unfinished business that haunts you. You are the only one who can accomplish this. You have the ability and can develop the expertise.

Summary

It is possible for you to show respect for your self-absorbed parent in interactions with him or her without agreeing with the parent's characterization of you or having to buy into the parent's denigrating comments about you. This chapter has presented a technique, reflective responding, that will enable you to mirror the expressed or unexpressed feeling of the parent without taking on any of the negativity embedded in the parent's message, or seeming to agree with it. It is helpful to practice giving a reflective response before adding your input.

Two essential components for building a better self—creativity and inspiration—were discussed, along with suggestions for how to initiate, increase, and enhance these for enriching your life. The final section addressed the cultivating and strengthening of your important relationships. The next and final chapter guides you in a process for additional healing for the wounds inflicted by your self-absorbed parent.

CHAPTER ACTIVITIES

Writing

Make a list of five inspirers that are low or no cost, and that can be easily accessed, and write a resolution to use one or more of these every day.

Drawing/Collage

Materials: A sheet of paper and a set of crayons, or felt markers, or colored pencils.

Draw the feeling you get when you are inspired, or feel uplifted, or are hopeful.

Visualization

Sit in silence, close your eyes, and allow an image of yourself as you wish to be to emerge. What do you look like? Facial expression? Posture? Body position? Are you smiling?

CHAPTER 10

You Can Do It:
Taking Charge of Your Self

Introduction

This final chapter has two parts. Each presents and summarizes how to overcome many of the negative outcomes you may have suffered from the self-absorbed parenting you received. Previous chapters described some of the possible impacts of the parental self-absorbed behaviors and attitudes and how the impact of these are still exerting their influences, and presented some suggested strategies and techniques that you could try to overcome the negative impacts of these on you.

The first part of this final chapter presents some information and guiding reflections to help you to begin to become aware of and understand some more of the forces that impacted and shaped your current self. This awareness and understanding can help you to take charge and develop the self you want to be, and will suggest where and how you can change. You can also gain a better understanding of how your current reactions and relationships are impacted by your earlier relationships and experiences, and this can help you start to be more objective in your perceptions, reactions, and responses instead of just reacting to the new in terms of the old.

The second part of this chapter focuses on the need to relinquish some fantasies, behaviors, and attitudes; how this may be accomplished; and an extension of the discussion of healing strategies and techniques to enhance your well-being. The chapter ends with a thirty-day plan for positive changes.

The Influence of Your Early Experiences

One approach to understanding the influence your early experiences had on your developing self is to examine some of your current behaviors, attitudes, and beliefs about yourself. This is especially helpful when those are troubling to you or to your relationships or are causing you to engage in possibly self-destructive behaviors.

Let's use three categories for examination: Helpless and Needy, Controlling and Rigid, and Self-Sacrificing and Resentful. These three categories may not capture all of your current behaviors, attitudes, and beliefs that are related to your early experiencing, but most will fall into one category. Following are some examples for each category.

The "Helpless and Needy" category includes the mistaken belief that you are unable to survive on your own and that you need someone to take care of you. Examine the following examples to see if these fit you or if you want to change this about yourself.

- You frequently request or expect others to take care of you, to do favors for you, or to attend to your welfare and well-being.

- You have failed relationships where you were overly attentive to or demanding of the other person.

- You easily feel isolated and alienated when you do not receive the attention you want.

These types of behaviors, attitudes, and beliefs were incorporated from your early experiences that emphasized your helplessness and dependency on others. While that was certainly true of you as an infant and child, it is not valid or helpful for you as an adult.

The "Controlling and Rigid" category refers to power needs as the basis for the behavior, attitudes, and beliefs. You are seeking to show that you are competent and adequate and that others must acknowledge this about you. Examine the following examples to determine if or how they may fit, their effect on your well-being and relationships, and if changes would be helpful.

- Winning is everything and I must do whatever it takes to win.

- No one has my well-being in mind, so it is up to me to ensure that others give me what I want or need.

- I like to play one-upmanship and to tease or taunt others.

This mindset was developed from your early experiences that are causing you to be protective and defensive of your self. You received messages that you were incompetent, inadequate, and not good enough.

The final category of "Self-Sacrificing and Resentful" has behaviors, attitudes, and beliefs that are using ingratiation to attain the appreciation and gratitude of others. In other words, survival is sought through taking care of others so that you will feel cared for. Here are some examples for you to examine:

- You have a need to receive constant appreciation and approval from others.

- You provide others with constant reminders of what you do for them and the sacrifices you make for others.

- You verbalize how you are taken for granted or minimized in spite of how much you give of yourself.

These and other similar behaviors, attitudes, and beliefs have ties to your early experiences where you received conscious and unconscious messages about your responsibility to take care of others but your efforts to do so went unrecognized and unappreciated, while any mistakes or lapses on your part were emphasized and you were blamed for not being good enough.

The next four sections expand on the influences of your early experiences on shaping your current self. They can be summed up as follows:

- Your parent had expectations for attitudes and behaviors that you unconsciously incorporated and acted on, and these continue to influence you in unexpected or unexplored ways.

- You received unfavorable comparisons with others by your parent about such things as your physical attractiveness, your intelligence, or your abilities.

- You feel the need to maintain a façade and to not reveal your real feelings.

- You feel that you have the responsibility to take care of others' emotional well-being and to ensure that they never feel distress.

These early messages have become so incorporated into your essential inner self that you may not even be aware of their existence until you take the time to reflect on them. They are an ingrained part of who you are, but were incorporated and identified without conscious intent. These continue to affect your self-perception today, and can play a role in determining the extent to which you feel guilty, can be easily wounded, or do not understand the limits of your responsibilities for others.

Unconscious Incorporation of Parental Expectations

Your forming self, when you were an infant and child, was very open and vulnerable. That meant that you were extremely alert and sensitive to signs of pleasure and displeasure from your parent or primary caretaker, and others around you. Everything you encountered was processed and sorted in terms of your essential inner self, and you were appropriately self-absorbed at that time. You took in voice tone, facial expressions, how you were physically handled, and other nonverbal messages that signaled how the other person felt about you, even before you had any notion of words and their meanings. This is why some nonverbal communications you receive today are interpreted the way they are by you. You were reinforced for expected behavior by nonverbal signs, such as smiles and a soft and intimate voice tone. As an infant and child, you valued these positive reactions as validations of your worth and value. These were also validations of your self-perception, that is, that you were as wonderful as you thought you were.

Reflection: Think about how you react when you encounter an unfamiliar situation. Do you observe what others are doing and take your cues from them? Are you alert to others' reactions to you, and do you take your cues from their positive and negative nonverbal communication? Are you wounded when you make a mistake, or when someone's nonverbal communication indicates disapproval? These could be some present-day associations with early learning about expected behaviors and attitudes.

Unfavorable Comparisons

Another early experience that can contribute to your current reactions, and even to some of your actions, is the unfavorable comparisons you may have received from your parent. This would be especially true if the comparisons portrayed you as inferior, inadequate, shameful, or unlovable. An example of the lingering effects is seen in the following reflection.

Reflection: Ask yourself, are you annoyed, hurt, or angered when others do or say something that indicates that they do not find your physical self to be attractive? Is your initial response a flash of irritation, embarrassment, or even hurt? If so, then the remarks are wounding, even if you are able to shrug them off, laugh, ignore them, or dismiss them. What you may be hearing and reacting to are old parental messages about your physical appearance.

Other examples of these old parental messages and their continuing impact and influence can be detected in your reactions when there is an inference, hint, or direct comment about your intelligence or abilities that seem to minimize or disparage these. These can arouse feelings of inadequacy, inferiority, shame, and unworthiness. These feelings often underlie the anger or rage that some people express when they think they are experiencing a put-down, or a perception that they are stupid or inept, or when someone tries to manipulate them, or they feel exploited. The resulting reaction, such as anger, can lead you to lash out at the offending person, to displace those feelings onto someone else, or even to buy in to the perception and berate yourself for not being better.

Maintaining a Façade

When the infant's and the child's true self does not receive acceptance and approval from the mother, or major caretaker, a false self emerges. If this happens continually, then the false self assumes dominance and is on display most or all of the time. That false self is reinforced and becomes the façade that is presented to the world. It becomes more difficult for the person to access the true self, and that person may have difficulty separating the two and begin to consciously accept the false self as the real self. The real self gets buried deeply and may even disappear from the consciousness.

Maintaining a conscious or unconscious façade can protect the true self from wounding. After all, it was or is not acceptable or approved of anyway, and needs all the protection it can get. The façade is used so that the self will not suffer, and that façade can become so prominent or ingrained that the person considers it to be the true self. Some indications of a possible false self as your façade are the following:

- Dismissing wounding experiences as being unimportant, such as trying to laugh off what someone said or did.

- Making sure that no one knows you are wounded, such as not letting your nonverbal behavior show that you were hurt.

- Suppressing your feelings aroused by a wounding comment or action, not even letting yourself be aware of being wounded.

- Pretending to be above it all.

This does not mean that the façade is wrong or inappropriate, as there can be times and situations where it is safer for you to hide your true feelings. What can be helpful is for you to admit to yourself that you are using a façade, and to stay in touch with how much you do use it. It is also helpful for you to examine yourself and see if your real self is known to you, if it is allowed to emerge, or if you don't even know your real self. If your true self is really unknown to you, or seldom allowed to emerge, you may be acting on an early parental message that reinforced your false self. Your challenge will be to find your true self, who you really are, and to build and reinforce it.

Reflection: Try to recall when you felt safe enough to let your real thoughts and feelings be known. Do you find that you seldom if ever allow this to happen? Are you aware of what your real feelings and thoughts are, or do you constantly try to hide these even from yourself?

Responsibility for the Emotional Well-Being of Others

It is easy to arouse your feelings of inadequacy, shame, and guilt if you believe that it is your responsibility to take care of others, and are in the habit of doing so. You may become wounded when others indicate they are uncomfortable or upset, when they cry, when they are angry, and so on. Somehow you have incorporated the notion that you are supposed to prevent this from happening, and you were not good enough, or failed to do so. Your thoughts about yourself can be something like, "I must be an awful person to let this happen." You may spend a considerable amount of time and effort taking care of other people you don't even know or like just because you are acting on this long-term, firmly entrenched old parental message that you are expected to take care of others.

Were you responsible for the physical or emotional well-being of your parent or parent figure, or even both parents? This is called parentification, where instead of the self-absorbed parent taking care of the child's well-being, the child is expected to assume responsibility for the parent's well-being, especially that parent's emotional well-being.

Reflection: Do you get upset when others seem to be upset and feel that you must do something to relieve their distress? Or feel that it is your fault that this happened in the first place? Are you still feeling responsible for your parents' well-being even though they are capable of taking care of themselves?

What Can Be Relinquished

Presented here are two categories for what can be relinquished: your fantasies and your self-absorbed behaviors and attitudes. Giving these up and letting go can be very freeing, and this makes room for more enriching and enduring things in your life.

Fantasies

Fantasies keep you longing for something that is unrealistic. They are energy sapping, and erode your time and resources that could be better used to work on your healing, growth, and development.

Reflection: Do you find yourself thinking about or imagining scenarios where your self-absorbed parent changes and can appreciate and value you, is empathic when you need them to be, apologizes for past actions, says something positive about you, does something to show their love for you, atones, or something similar?

If you resonate with any of the examples in that reflection, you have fantasies about your parent. Self-absorbed parents are unlikely to change because they see no reason to change. They think they are "right" in their perceptions, behaviors, and attitudes and that you are "wrong" if you differ or challenge them. It's been that way all of your life, but you just keep hoping, wishing, and yearning for them to change and that hasn't happened. You cannot make it happen, and the time you spend fantasizing about that, even when you think those times are few, takes away time that you could be using for more constructive thoughts and plans.

How can you give up this fantasy? You may never be able to entirely relinquish your longing and yearning, but you can stop yourself when you find that you are thinking about the parent changing, or getting frustrated when the parent does or says hurtful things and doesn't notice the negative impact on you, or when you become narcissistically wounded or enraged at that parent's behavior or attitude. You can interrupt your thought, hurt, or rage with a simple phrase such as one of the following:

- I'm still expecting the impossible or the improbable.

- Leopards don't change their spots.

- I'm trying to relate to a wall.

- I'm adding to my frustration or hurt, because I am still yearning and hoping that my parent will change.

Another strategy to interrupt a fantasy is to use a distraction. In other words, visualize or do something pleasant like one of the following:

- A visual distraction, such as a cat or dog video or a sporting event.

- An auditory distraction, such as music, sounds in your environment, laughing at a joke.

- Inviting odors, such as flowers, a bakery, or perfumed soap.

- Tactile sensations, such as running your hand over a smooth stone, stroking silk, noticing how water feels on your skin.

- Creating something, such as making a collage.

- Reading a magazine or book.

- Writing the great American novel.

You probably have your own unique set of distractions. They can be very helpful to interrupt fantasies.

Change Self-Absorbed Behaviors and Attitudes

Just because you cannot see your behaviors and attitudes that are reflective of self-absorption doesn't mean that you don't have any. Assume that you do, and that you want to change these or grow in more constructive ways. Understand that change is gradual, difficult at times, and may not always be received well by others. Following are some possible changes for the various self-absorbed behaviors and attitudes.

Grandiosity can be reduce and managed better if you can refrain from taking on too much and expecting to do all of it as well as you do when there is less to do. You can focus on trying to have realistic expectations of yourself and of others.

Arrogance can result from grandiosity and it occurs when you feel superior. Yes, you may have some talents and capabilities and attributes that others do not have, but you may also either consciously or unconsciously convey to others that you feel superior. Become more aware of your personal limitations and cultivate modesty and humbleness about your capabilities and attributes.

Contempt can also result from grandiosity and allow you to be contemptuous of anyone you think is not up to your standards. Try to not dismiss others who are not as talented or understanding or who do not have the resources that you do. Cultivate an appreciation of others as being unique, different, and worthwhile.

Acting from an impoverished ego can cause you to be overly sensitive to any hint of perceived criticism or blame, to engage in self-defeating behaviors, and to look to others to take care of you. The impoverished ego is the flip side of grandiosity, where you can perceive everything as being about you. It can be helpful to understand that everything is not personally directed at you, others are not always critical of you, nor are you to blame about everything.

Whining, carping, and complaining occur when things are not going as you want them to and when others are not doing what you want or expect them to do. You may think that you are only expressing your thoughts and feelings, but it may not be received that way. You can reduce the distress you may be feeling if you can become more independent and self-sufficient, and not rely on others to either do what you want, or to ensure that things are as you want them to be. Do it for yourself.

Attention-seeking behaviors can keep you in the spotlight and help make you feel important. Instead of seeking attention, you can experiment with restraining your actions to let others have the spotlight, and see how you feel and how others treat you. You may find that you can be content with less attention than before.

Admiration-hungry actions result from a need to have others recognize and appreciate you. Some ways that you can change what you do and why you do them are to try and do what you see needs to be done without expecting anything; you act because you want to. Try to not tell others all of the things you do for them or for others, as this is seeking appreciation. Some people seek admiration for their suffering and are quick to let others know how much they have to endure, and you may want to check your behavior to stop or reduce this behavior.

An entitlement attitude can cause you to be indifferent to others' opinions or needs. Some people with this attitude are pushy and denigrating of others, and expect preferential treatment at all time. You probably cannot see this in yourself, but you may want to try to not become angry or hurt when you don't receive the deference you feel is due you. Try to monitor your expectations of what others are supposed to do, and do not have tantrums or sulk when you don't receive what you expect to receive.

Exploitation is also probably unconscious, and you may not be aware of how you use manipulation, seduction, or intimidation to get what you want or to have others do what you want them to do. Reflect on your actions and try to appreciate others as being separate and distinct from you, realizing that they are entitled to say no to your requests or demands and that they do not have to do what you want them to do. Reflect on and monitor any tendency to try to manipulate, control, seduce, or coerce others, especially those closest to you, and do what you can to reduce and eliminate those tendencies.

Envy can erode your self-confidence and self-efficacy. It is not a productive use of your time to envy what others have or can do. It is much more rewarding to capitalize on the assets you do have and to work to get what you want. It could be helpful to reflect not only on how getting what someone else has would benefit you, but also on what you might have to give up to get what the other person has. You may find that you are happier and more productive when you strengthen your inner essential self and use the assets and resources that you do have, including some that you may be overlooking.

Emptiness at the core of oneself is something that is difficult to address. Mere activities, multiple and not satisfying relationships, and the like will not fill the emptiness. This is best addressed working with a competent mental health professional to help you develop your life's meaning and purpose.

Lack of empathy negatively affects your relationships. Empathy essentially comes from within you, where you have strong psychological boundary strength that enables you to enter the world of the other person, and are able to feel what that person feels without becoming enmeshed or overwhelmed by the intensity of that person's feelings. You may want to at least try responding empathically, even if you are not feeling what the other person is feeling. For example, you may know that someone is sad but you are not feeling the sadness. Your empathic response would acknowledge that the other person is sad. You can do the same with other feelings, and make your response to them one that identifies the feeling they have or are trying to communicate.

These are just some of the self-absorbed behaviors and attitudes that can be reduced, eliminated, or changed. You may not be aware of those that you have and exhibit, but you can nevertheless work to try and change them just in case they do exist.

Grow and Thrive

Letting go of unproductive and self-defeating behaviors and attitudes is only a first step in growing and thriving. You will also have to adopt some constructive and self-building behaviors and attitudes. Other chapters have suggestions and techniques for your building that will be helpful, and you are encouraged to review and try some of those. This final section focuses on growing, thriving, and healing by building a winning attitude and increasing your happy moments, along with a thirty-day plan for a more balance in your life.

A Winning Attitude

The negative effects of your self-absorbed parent may lead you to perceive yourself as inadequate, inferior, ineffective, and a whole host of other self-defeating thoughts and attitudes. Even today as an adult you may berate yourself for any of the following:

- Making a mistake, especially when others are aware of your mistake.

- Competing for something, and someone else comes out ahead of you.

- Wanting to achieve something and not achieving it.

- Having an idea, a thought, or a creation such as a book manuscript rejected.

- Not being selected for a club, a sorority or fraternity, or the college of your choice.

- Losing an argument.

- Not being able to get someone to do what you want them to do.

You may begin to perceive yourself as fatally flawed, think that others also see these flaws and will reject or destroy you, and that you will never be able to overcome these fatal flaws. While it is certainly true that you, like everyone else, have inadequacies and can be ineffective at times, it is also true that these can be addressed and modified, and that other positive assets are available or can be developed. It is more about you having a realistic and winning attitude than it is about failure and flaws.

A realistic winning attitude does not mean dismissing or ignoring mistakes; instead, it will allow you to learn from these, to better assess your goals and needs, and to take appropriate actions to raise the possibility of your success.

A winning attitude incorporates all or most of the following:

1. The primary focus is on the task at hand and self-performance, not on the opponent, or on barriers. For example, in interactions with your self-absorbed parent, your primary focus can be on managing your feelings, not on what the parent is doing or saying.

2. An ability to visualize success. Some of the "Activities" in previous chapters suggested visualizations that could be helpful. You may also find it helpful to visualize what you would consider as success in the relationship with your self-absorbed parent and for interactions with that parent.

3. Winners are always seeking improvement. Reflect on what you could improve, such as becoming more understanding and empathic with your partner, reducing or eliminating some of your self-absorption, or making more of an effort to engage in altruistic acts.

4. Use positive thoughts, encouragers, and affirmations. Be kind to yourself. When you start to berate yourself for a mistake or a perceived flaw, take a moment to say something like, "I'll do better," and let the negative thought go. You don't have to forget your mistake or flaw, but neither do you have to dwell on it and make yourself more miserable.

5. Do not become devastated when you lose. Winners do not like losing and are disappointed, but they do not become devastated when they lose. Try to have a more moderate reaction to losing, whether it is a parking

space or an argument, and to not think of yourself as flawed because of that one loss.

6. Most of all, winners are confident about their selves. They are mindful of their strengths and weaknesses, understand that they can continue to grow and develop, and are willing to work to get better at whatever they are choosing to do or be.

7. A deep desire to not lose can fuel a winning attitude, encourage you to take positive steps to develop the aspects of yourself needed to win, and enable you to objectively assess the barriers and constraints you may encounter. But first you have to define winning for yourself and assess how much you do not want to lose. Also, since there are many aspects to your life, all of these need to be considered and what winning would mean for you in each of these.

Everyone wants to win, to be successful, to come out on top, and to not be perceived as a loser. But winning, success, and being on top are defined by the individual and these definitions are unique to each person's personality, upbringing, and life circumstances. Your definitions also shift across time and depending on your experiences, so that what defined winning when you were a child or adolescent is not how you define it as an adult.

Wanting to win, working for success, and having a winning attitude are all very positive and can make significant contributions to boosting your mood. Care must be taken, however, to monitor your actions and perceptions so that you do not exploit or manipulate others to get what you want to win, or to use any means necessary in pursuit of winning. A winning attitude is a belief in yourself, confidence in your efficacy, and an understanding of your limitations.

Increase Your Happy Moments

Few people can be happy all of the time, but all of us can experience happy moments. What is proposed here is that you begin to collect some happy moments, so that when you are down, you can reflect on those moments as well as trying to increase these in your life.

Happy moments lift spirits, provide hope, and can increase your physical and psychological well-being. These are usually brief and transitory, although we may wish them to be more lasting. Negative moods, such as being demoralized or depressed, can be endured better if you can recall some of your happier moments.

What can constitute a happy moment? See if any of the following could work for you as a happy moment:

- An unexpected recognition of your accomplishment.

- Being present when a family member accomplishes something important or gratifying, for example having a child, receiving a sport or academic achievement award, or getting a promotion at work.

- When your solution to a problem works or produces a positive result.

- Hearing that you got the job you were seeking, or a raise or a promotion.

- Being recruited for membership in something you want or feel is important.

- Seeing a creative product of yours on display.

- Finishing a complex, long, involved project.

- Receiving a gift from someone significant to you.

- Realizing that you are getting better, recovering, or growing.

- Feeling at peace with yourself.

No one but you can define your happy moments. These are just suggestions to get you started to think about what gives you a feeling of happiness, if only for that moment or a short period of time.

Reflection: What do you do when you are happy: smile, twirl, dance, sing, whistle, or what? When was the last time you had a happy moment?

A Thirty-Day Plan

We close with a suggested thirty-day plan to increase your sense of well-being, with some activities that will guide you. These were developed with the assumption that you would not have a lot of time to spend on any one of them, and that most suggested activities can be completed in ten minutes or less if all materials are available.

Week	Goal	Activities
1.	Find beauty everyday.	a. Locate three things in your favorite color each day for a week. b. Visualize a happy place and draw it. c. Fix a meal with three bright or pleasing colors, flavors, and odors on each of three days.
2.	Get organized.	a. Discard three things from your home or work environment every day for a week. b. Clean something every day for a week. This can be a small cleaning task. c. Declutter a drawer, table top, or the like each day.
3.	Create a product.	a. Draw loops on a piece of paper and color in some of the loops. b. Write your name as large as you can on a sheet of paper, then trace around the letters with a colored pencil on both sides of the letter, and draw little leaves or flowers by your name. c. Make a collage every day.
4.	Move.	a. March in place each day for one or more minutes. b. Dance with or without music for three to five minutes. c. Take a walk for ten or more minutes each day.

Other activities that may be helpful:

- Reflect on where you are and where you want to be.

- Give people who are close to you the gift of your attention and admiring comments; recognize and tell them about one or more of their strengths.

- Practice gratitude for what you have, such as your health, relationships, things, possibilities.

- Let go of envy, jealousy, hatred, and anything that is toxic for your well-being.

- Examine your "becauses," such as "I can't because..." or "I must because..." to determine how realistic these are or if you are perceiving barriers that do not have to exist.

- Resolve that you will not commit any negative acts, such as mocking, taunting, denigrating, bullying, seducing, manipulating, or coercing.

- Resolve that you will commit positive acts, such as smiling, saying hello, being civil and courteous.

- Balance happiness and responsibility, duty and principles, self and others' needs, denial and reality.

You now have a lot of information; suggestions for how you can heal and grow; guidance for how to better understand yourself; and a number of tools for building your inner self and becoming the person you want to be. I'll end with wishing you the best for now and for the future!

References

Brown, N. 2002. *Whose Life Is It Anyway? When to Stop Taking Care of Their Feelings and Start Taking Care of Your Own.* Oakland, CA: New Harbinger Publications.

Brown, N. 2006. *Coping with Infuriating, Mean, Critical People: The Destructive Narcissistic Pattern.* Westport, CT: Praeger.

Hatfield, E., J. T. Cacioppo, and R. L. Rapson. 1994. *Emotional Contagion.* Cambridge, UK: Cambridge University Press.

Kohut, H. 1977. *The Restoration of the Self.* New York: International Universities Press.

Mahler, M., and M. Furer. 1968. *On Human Symbiosis and the Vicissitudes of*

Individuation: Infantile Psychoses. New York: International Universities Press.

Nina W. Brown, EdD, LPC, DFAGPA, received her doctorate from the College of William and Mary, and is a professor and eminent scholar of counseling at Old Dominion University in Norfolk, VA. Brown is past president of the Society of Group Psychology and Group Psychotherapy, and current president of the Group Specialty Council. She is author of twenty-seven books, including *Loving the Self-Absorbed* and *Whose Life is it Anyway?*

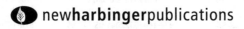

MORE BOOKS *from*
NEW HARBINGER PUBLICATIONS

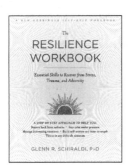
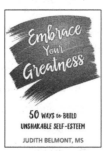